The
10-Day
Relaxation
Plan

The 10-Day Relaxation Plan

Dr ERIC TRIMMER

PIATKUS

© 1984 Dr Eric Trimmer

First published in 1984
by Judy Piatkus (Publishers) Limited of London

British Library Cataloguing in Publication Data
Trimmer, Eric
  The 10 day relaxation plan.
  1. Relaxation
  I. Title
  613.7'9   RA785

  ISBN 0-86188-416-7

Designed by Susan Ryall
Drawings by Françoise Trainaud

Typeset by Tradespools Ltd, Frome, Somerset
Printed in Great Britain by Mackays of Chatham Ltd

How to use this book   7   Contents

The 10-day relaxation plan

Understanding the stress in your life

More ways to relax

How stress causes illness

Everybody is affected by anxiety, tension or stress, but because we are all made differently stress affects us differently too. How you use this book depends on the sort of person you are and exactly what your problem is.

In the 10-day plan there are three schemes to suit three main types of people. Study the characteristics of the groups carefully (pages 16 to 17), but don't worry if you do not fit a group exactly. If in doubt, choose the course which you think you will most *enjoy* following – i.e. the course which you think suits you best. It is always possible to move to a different course if you feel that other techniques would suit you better. In fact, as the course proceeds you may well learn something about yourself which makes you want to explore a slightly different scheme. That's fine too.

Group 1 is loosely based on yoga and autogenics; Group 2 on muscle relaxation; Group 3 explores massage-induced relaxation. All groups learn the essential relaxation breathing techniques, and 'borrow' routines from each other from time to time so that everybody can have some appreciation of the other methods of relaxation.

You will begin to feel the benefits of learning to relax from the very first day, and by the time you reach the end of the course you will have put together a tailor-made routine which will allow you to relax at will and help you overcome stress. The course is planned to take ten days to complete. But all effective plans are flexible, and this applies to the 10-day relaxation plan. Only move on to the next day when you feel ready.

Don't be surprised if your technique changes gradually with practice. Expect this to happen and use a technique that really works for you. Reject one that doesn't. Learn to trust your feelings and instincts about this. You will probably find an individual relaxation trigger which could be something incredibly simple, but which will work for you – and make you feel really pleased that you made the effort to discover relaxation.

You may opt to go straight to the 10-day relaxation plan. Or you may prefer to learn more about the cause of your anxiety first, as it is very important to recognize what causes tension if you are to take action against it. In that case you should start at Chapter 4. However, if you are one of the vast numbers of people who are suffering from stress-related diseases, then obviously you should begin at the end of the book and refer back to the parts of the 10-day plan which will benefit you most.

Some people do not like the idea of following the 10-day self-help programme on their own – the whole concept is too boring or lonely – and they may be attracted to the 'Relax with a friend' section. This is based on body massage and muscle relaxation, and encourages two people to alternate as 'giver' and 'taker'. This method can be very successful for those who do things better as 'couples'.

The power of faith healing is of intense interest to some people, while those of a more scientific persuasion will find the modern biofeedback machines, where your *degree* of stress is monitored, more interesting. There is also a chapter for people who want to relax and get a good night's sleep without having to resort to sleeping pills at every bedtime.

Everybody, except victims of bad depression, can learn to relax and feel better for the experience. In a way it is a bit like learning to swim. To start with you have to concentrate on the strokes and work at them for a while. Then suddenly everything clicks into place – and you can't understand why you did not master it years ago.

Eric Trimmer
London, 1984

The 10-Day Relaxation Plan

CHAPTER 1

Introduction

It is important to realize that being under stress and being relaxed are two perfectly natural states of everyday living. A certain amount of stress is necessary to get things done. It has a 'get up and go' function that we all need. But too much stress can be harmful. In fact, half the population of the Western world will eventually suffer from stress-induced diseases, mostly when they are in their 50s and their 60s.

However, somewhere between the stressed state and the relaxed state is a midway position known as *homeostasis*, and if stress is countered with homeostasis, then it will do no harm.

Homeostasis means 'like standing', and it is perhaps one of the most recent jargon words to enter the language of alternative or complementary medicine. It has a place in this book on relaxation, however, because it describes an admirable state of mind and body in which one has the inclination and ability to 'stand and stare', thus making a therapeutic pause in the sometimes traumatic experiences of everyday life. The way to achieve homeostasis is to learn to relax.

Some people find it easy to recognize stress and know how to relax. Others don't. But luckily relaxation can be taught. Learning how to relax has nothing to do with entering a zombie-like state or getting so drunk on relaxation that ambition, drive, intelligent risk-taking, persistence and stamina get submerged in a sea of inactivity and sloth. There will be no dimming of consciousness when you relax, but you will find that emotional disturbances can no longer bother you.

Learning to relax is powerfully therapeutic. Probably the first thing you will notice when you start to relax properly is that your powers of concentration will improve. Small irritations will no longer be enervating. You won't sigh so much, and when you get tired that tiredness will be a healthy tiredness to be enjoyed. No longer will you have to whip your body into action all the time.

These beneficial effects can be felt very quickly if you follow one of the three regimes described on pages 15 to 93. The relaxation programme includes a self-selection technique in which you, the reader, pick the easiest way for *you* to relax. You will discover what exercise or routine will trigger the relaxation response in you, and by the end of the 10-day course you should be able to relax at will and cope with tension in all its forms.

Stress is the 'disease' of the late 20th century. It affects every system of the body. It affects the way our bodies function in what appears to be an arbitrary, almost random way. Some people seem to cope with stress – others crack up. This fact can be understood if you examine what the psychologists call *coping skills*. Good coping skills are part inborn and part learned. For instance, they are enjoyed more often by those who have been fortunate enough to have experienced good mothering. Security at home and at work helps too. The man or woman who lives in a stable society and who enjoys a modicum of success, reward and acclaim will cope with a degree of stress that will damage the less well placed. Poor coping skills, which mean not being able to take even moderate degrees of stress, are also linked to defective education, low social status and feelings of being low in the pecking order of life.

It is worth taking a look at a couple of case histories to see how differently people can react to stress.

William had shot up the ladder of promotion in his chosen profession rapidly. At 30 he had a large mortgage, a hefty overdraft, hire purchase commitments, three children and a loving wife. One day he found that his company was being taken over by another firm and that his job was to disappear in the New Year. Naturally he experienced a nasty shock, but still felt that his assets outnumbered his liabilities and that he could *cope* with the situation. Within a few months he had found a job (less well paid), and was busy getting his life together again.

Robin's problems started as a result of a car accident and an inability, subsequently, to drive. His self-employed job evaporated overnight, but his wife was working and they had no family commitments. Theoretically he should have *coped* with this unkind knock from the hand of fate, but somehow he did not. He described his marriage as a happy one, but clearly he and his wife were much more interested in their own careers and activities than in marriage as a lifestyle. His sudden loss of status and security had a profound effect on him: he lost his powers of concentration, his drive, his sense of humour and his peace of mind. His inability to *cope* with his problems, rather than anything else, lowered him into the depths of depression.

But before shoulders are shrugged too despondently or hopelessly, it has been shown that coping skills can be raised by training and by a particular and interesting form of discipline. Part of that training and discipline is what this book is about.

Discipline is a word that has been considerably ill used. Its basic meaning is 'instruction imparted to scholars' – disciples, if you like. And this training and discipline teaches how to master the ill effects of stress and can be effective for everyone, the socially and emotionally deprived included. Learning the *discipline* of relaxation is the name of the game, and anyone can play. Choose the relaxation scheme most suited to your age and characteristics and start the 10-day course today.

The Relaxation Response

All through this book I shall be talking about the *relaxation response*. This is a sort of shorthand phrase to describe the many changes in the body's functioning that are brought about by learning to relax. Stress and tension produce secondary effects on the body, and the fact is that the body would not perform at all well in a stressful state without these physiological changes; they redistribute our life's blood and prime our whole neuro-muscular system for action. The relaxation response is characterized by its own physiology too. The heart rate slows, the blood pressure falls, the metabolic function of the body switches into low gear – all the cells in the body become less responsive to the stress hormones that constantly circulate and prime it. In other words, homeostasis takes over.

The importance of learning to relax has been realized by man, perhaps subconsciously, from the earliest of times. Often in the past the method used was surrounded by ritual and acted out from complex codes. But now we have broken the code and can examine the facts about relaxation techniques in a fair amount of detail. We can even choose the type of relaxation training which is best suited to us.

Much of the early deciphering of relaxation techniques was done at Harvard University's Medical School by Professor Herbert Benson and his team. As a result of painstaking research, four basic components have been separated which, when combined and properly blended to suit the individual, bring about the much desired and therapeutic *relaxation response*. These four components must be uppermost in your mind whenever you settle yourself to relax.

1. BODY POSITION AND CLOTHING

The first component is to assume a comfortable and sometimes specific or naturalistic body position. This is *not* a sleep-inducing position. It can range widely – from lying on the floor to sitting in a chair – and should be closely tailored to the individual. It should match his or her age and personality, and take into consideration any personal preferences, quirks or even disabilities.

Wearing loose and comfortable clothing will also help you to programme yourself towards learning the relaxation response.

2. THE PLACE

To start with, a quiet and private environment is necessary. Beginners should choose somewhere behind a closed door and away from the sound of the telephone or doorbell. The well-disciplined will be able to relax almost anywhere – in buses, trains, taxis and aeroplanes. The exercises should not be carried out within two hours of a substantial meal as relaxation does not come easily to a full stomach – sleep is the more likely result.

3. REPETITION

The third basic ingredient of the relaxation response is an element of repetition. The ritualistic use of the words of a prayer charac-terizes almost all societies, but only recently has it been shown that prayers can have a psychological as well as a religious component to them. A sound or a phrase which is often repeated serves a secular purpose and need not be meaningful in any way. (Some relaxation cults resort to humming or buzzing noises.) From the Sanskrit comes the word *mantra*, which means an instrument of thought. Usually, but not always, a mantra is a sacred text or passage from the Vedas, such a prayer or incantation being chosen for the individual by a 'master'. But you may, with equal effect, repeat your own name – as did the poet Tennyson – or use some other phrase. (Suitable phrases are suggested in the 10-day course, and more information on the mantra can be found in Chapter 3.)

4. THOUGHT CONTROL

The final corner stone is the adoption of what is usually referred to as a *dismissive attitude* during the period of relaxation. This is often, for both the beginner and the more experienced, the main stumbling block. Learning thought-control is difficult, and to a large extent it is the area where active relaxation *training* is most necessary. But there are various ways in which this dissociation from everyday thoughts and dreams may be achieved. The most effective is by a process of *redirecting* the attention *away* from general thought patterns.

It is very nearly impossible to do two things at once. We can be caught up in our thoughts, intellectually aroused, or even bound up with frantic day dreaming and fantasy. These are all conditions that are the antithesis of calmness – and death to the relaxation response. But it is possible to direct our 'attention' (if that is the right word to use) towards what might be called our vegetative self. One useful and effective way to do this – and this is what I shall be concentrating on in certain sections of the 10-day course – is by learning *muscular relaxation* and, in all groups, specially worked out *breathing techniques*. These are catalysts in the development of the dismissive attitude.

An example of relaxation breathing techniques tailored to a very specialized subject is of course Dr Grantly Dick-Read's relaxation techniques used to facilitate natural childbirth. These breathing-dominated techniques concentrate the mind on the body's automatic (autonomic) functions and the deep degree of relaxation experienced, if properly applied, studied and practised, blocks out, or dismisses, the immediate appreciation of pain. In other words, concentrating on the breathing techniques throughout childbirth makes the pain of secondary importance while the mother produces her baby.

CHAPTER 2

The 10-day relaxation plan has been worked out with the average person in mind, but all of us are different and sometimes it is necessary to spend a couple of days sampling one particular section or another. Keep your plan flexible. It is far better to give yourself a chance to assimilate the day's relaxation teaching and be confident that you are happy with it before you move on than to rush through the course in the minimum of 10 days and maybe not achieve the desired result.

Each day's relaxation training takes between 20 and 30 minutes to complete, and ideally it should be practised twice during the course of the day. Once learned, the exercises are revised and then built into your own individual relaxation routine.

Choosing your method

Learning to relax is not a push-button process that can be switched on in the same way by everyone. We are all made differently and stress affects us differently as well. To some extent age comes into this, but so also do other characteristics.

I suggest three groups of students for my three rather different relaxation programmes:

GROUP 1: This technique usually works best for younger age groups (15–35).

GROUP 2: This is mainly for the 35–60 age group, but some from this age group will find Group 1 techniques more attractive than Group 2 methods, even if they are nearer 40 than 20.

GROUP 3: Most of those who use Group 3 techniques to relax are over 60, but some of that age group cheerfully opt for Group 1. For some, a disability will direct them towards this group despite their more tender years.

Spend a little time looking at the group identification chart on the following two pages before you go ahead and learn to relax in 10 days. But don't be put off if you find that you do not fit precisely into any of the three groups. The aim of the programme is for you to discover the technique that best triggers the relaxation response in you. If in doubt, start by following the course you think you will most enjoy; and change if it does not work for you.

GROUP **1**	This group will consist mostly of people in the 15–35 age group, with the following characteristics:	They have muscles and bones that are strong, and joints that work well and are fully flexible. They feel better after exercise and like out-of-doors activity. Many are active sports people.
GROUP **2**	Mostly comprised of people in the 35–60 age group, with the following characteristics:	They have muscles that feel tired the day *after* exertion. Exercise does not stimulate or improve their sense of well-being very much. They enjoy good powers of concentration, but tend to put off doing things.
GROUP **3**	Mostly the over-60 age group, with the following characteristics:	There is some physical disability impinging on the lifestyle of most people in this group. Physical exercise tires them and tends to make them feel worse and exhausted. Their concentration often wanders, as does their attention.

They have difficulty in concentrating at times, and are easily upset by minor things going wrong.

There is a tendency to jumpiness and nervousness, and they often feel on edge, irritable, excitable.

They may over-indulge in food, drink, tobacco.

They experience few sleep problems and have a good tolerance to heat and cold.

Usually they feel understretched and often believe they could do better.

Symptoms of stress are rare, but when they do develop include palpitation (heart thumping), headaches.

GROUP 1

They are reasonably phlegmatic and not easily disturbed by minor upsets but resent Fate's unkindnesses.

They are not unduly nervous, but unsolved problems remain very much in the background of the mind and haunt them.

They are generally set in their ways, but feel they could change.

A difficulty in getting to sleep is common, and they dislike extremes of weather.

They would like to do better and be more successful.

They may well have heard about, or worried about, or suffered, a stress illness (e.g. peptic ulcer or hypertension).

GROUP 2

An accepting attitude towards disappointments and disability is often evident.

They are fairly set in their ways and are not flexible as far as changes in ideas are concerned.

This group usually gets to sleep easily but also wakes easily and early.

They are often upset by cold weather.

Most people in this group feel that they have more or less got where they wanted to.

Symptoms of stress are quite common (e.g. frequent palpitation, excessive sweating, breathing difficulties).

GROUP 3

Day One

GROUP 1

Preliminaries

This relaxation scheme is loosely based on yoga and autogenic principles. The routines should be performed twice daily, preferably at set times. Select a suitable place in which to carry out your relaxation programme, and try to use the same place throughout the 10 days. Wear loose clothes, and no shoes. (See page 12.)

You may find it curious that a book on relaxation techniques finds itself using what may seem very like gymnastic exercises. Chronic stress is, however, reflected in the way in which we stand, sit, work and generally conduct our lives. You could almost say that stress imprints itself on the whole of our muscular skeletal system. The successful osteopath appreciates this and spends a considerable part of his time attempting to remedy these stress-induced postural problems.

Stress may focus itself quite acutely on one particular body function. Frederick Matthias Alexander was an actor who suddenly found himself trying to cope with just about the worst stress problem that an actor has to face – the loss of his voice on stage. As a result of self-analysis he found that he could get over his speech difficulty by reorientating his posture while acting. He became so interested in the applications of his discovery that he devoted the rest of his life to teaching people to 'unlearn' their bad stress-induced postural habits. In the 10-day course we also explore the possibilities of unlearning bad postural habits.

Yoga component

1. STAND, STRETCH AND BREATHE

The idea in this first exercise is to try to feel taller and to learn rhythmic breathing.

a. Stand naturally, perhaps in front of a long mirror, with legs together and arms by your sides; ideally feet should be bare so that the toes can grip the floor.

b. Breathe in and out through the nose, counting one-and-two-and-three as you breathe in, and actively attempting to increase your height by at least an inch (2.5 cm).

Day One

GROUP

1

c. Pause – and exhale (breathe out). Let your height go back to normal at the end of a one-and-two-and-three – pause – exhalation.

To start with, on the first two or three inhalations, the period 'and three' will feel forced and you will feel that no more air is going into the lungs. Gradually you will adapt to 'three' so that the one-and-two-and-three count will become much more equal and effective. As you breathe in you will flatten your stomach, and your shoulders will rise with your chest. *Concentrate* on elongating your spine as you breathe in.

Repeat five times.

Stand naturally.

Breathe in: one-and-two-and-three – pause. Concentrate on elongating spine.

Breathe out: one-and-two-and-three – pause. Return to normal height at end of count.

19

GROUP

1

2. LEG BALANCE AND BREATHE

a. Take up the same posture and again 'get tall' while breathing rhythmically.

b. This time, on the first one-and-two-and-three – pause, lift the left leg off the floor and bring the left thigh to right angles to the body. To start with, some instability will be experienced and the right toes will be actively gripping the floor. There may also be some wobbling at the ankle or knee of the right leg.

c. Allow the leg to return to the floor.

Repeat three to five times with the left leg. As you get used to this, *concentrate* on getting taller with each leg raise, and as the leg is replaced *concentrate* on its heaviness and lack of tension compared with the right leg's tense and active condition as it strains to keep your balance.

Next, repeat with the other leg. Right-handed people will find that standing on the left leg is more difficult, and more wobbling will be evident until the toes learn to get a better grip on the floor and the muscles learn to compensate.

a	b	c

Stand naturally and get tall while breathing rhythmically.	Breathe in: one-and-two-and-three – pause as you lift left leg. Concentrate on getting taller.	Breathe out: one-and-two-and-three, replacing left foot at end of count. Concentrate on leg's heaviness and lack of tension compared with right leg.

Autogenic component

Autogenics means instructions made to yourself by yourself. It focuses attention to one part of the body. The first four sessions of autogenic relaxation should last about 20 minutes. Do not attempt to time check during the session, but make a note to expand or contract the session next day with 20 minutes in mind. Quite soon you will become remarkably adept at timing your autogenics. In these early sessions breathing should be natural and not in any way stylized or controlled.

a. To achieve the relaxation response choose a comfortable body position and a quiet place (see page 12), and note the time you start. Add a mantra component by saying to yourself, 'I am relaxed and at peace with myself'. Repeat five times.

b. Then focus mentally on your right arm, *concentrating* on how heavy it feels. Indulge yourself in this feeling of heaviness. When obtrusive outside thoughts intrude repeat the mantra and concentrate again on heaviness. After a few minutes move your attention to the left arm, again going back to the mantra when concentration wanders.

c. Gradually move to other 'heavy' areas: legs, head, shoulders, and finally pelvis. To start with the mantra will be used quite frequently.

Move on to Day Two regime only when you are ready to. Nothing is gained by hurry in these experiences.

Day One

GROUP

2

Preliminaries

Relaxation in this group responds best to muscle tension reduction combined with smooth rhythmic breathing. Some tense people, however, find that a period of physical activity before bringing about the relaxation response helps the whole process, and so a brisk walk, a gentle or graduated jog, or the *Aeroplane* yoga-type exercises detailed on pages 36 and 37 may be useful.

For *all* relaxation sessions follow the relaxation response components 1 and 2, outlined on page 12. Lying flat on the floor on a couple of blankets is an excellent body position for this group. (A routine is always to be preferred as everyone's body responds automatically to habit, and after a few days much of your *learned* relaxation will be automatically conditioned. Your relaxation room, the time of day and your general surroundings will automatically set the scene for the relaxation response.)

Your sense of *commitment* will determine how successful you are in learning the natural benefit of relaxation. The onus of success lies entirely with you and achievement is available to anyone who commits themself to the programme. Talking other people into trying to master the relaxation response often proves unrewarding.

Muscle relaxation

Muscle relaxation is the key to this particular programme and a few minutes spent defining relaxation in its special relationship to muscle tension is worth-while.

To start with, you must grasp the idea of a two-way link between emotions and what is happening to the muscles throughout your body. Consider the simple example of fear. When we experience the sensation of fear one of the automatic responses of the body is to increase muscle tension – to get us ready for fight or flight (see also Chapter 4). This is the first part of the two-way link. What is less commonly realized is the second part: if we start at the muscle end of the emotion or feeling of fear rather than at the brain end, and if muscle tension is reduced, then the experience of fear is also reduced.

I have taken fear as a simple everyday emotion, but of course in practice emotions and feelings are complex and I will examine them

in more detail later in the book. For the time being let us stick with this simple example and examine further the relationship between mind and muscle. Unless it is understood *how* relaxation of muscle can bring about relaxation of mind you may be tempted to dismiss the whole thing as a bit of pseudo-scientific mumbo jumbo.

Doctors and scientists stick labels on certain bodily functions and thus complex medical words evolve. Although these words give those who use them regularly a fair idea of what they are talking about, they mean little or nothing to the general reader. This is a pity because the people who coined the words knew *exactly* what they meant to say. One such word is *proprioceptive*. This adjective is used scientifically to decribe nerve impulses that are generated from *within* (inside) the body. Proprioceptive impulses of the greatest importance are generated in muscles and around tendons and joints.

A main function of these proprioceptive impulses is to tell you, for instance, what position your leg is in when you have your eyes shut. These impulses give accurate information when the forces of gravity are acting on you (e.g. when your [heavy] foot is touching a [rigid] floor) but so cleverly are they tuned that in no-gravity situations (e.g. in a swimming pool) your proprioceptive impulses still tell you exactly where your limbs are and what your body generally is doing under water, even though you cannot feel gravity working on it in the usual way.

Having understood what the modern medical scientist means by proprioceptive, adding as it does to the two-way nerve-muscle concept, let us return for a moment to the word proprioceptive and the concept of a proprioceptive muscle-nerve state. The word *proprium*, related to the word property, also means the *essential nature* of something, or (and this seems most important) its *selfhood*.

This concept gives us insight into the nature of the body's response to muscular relaxation. The relaxed muscle feeds information about its relaxed state to the mind, which is very relevant to the *selfhood* at that moment. Experiments have shown that the relaxed muscle and the relaxed self go together, and this is only logical.

On Day One you will begin to learn about the contribution of muscle relaxation to the whole body, and you will also learn how through *selfhood manipulation* at this muscular level you can feel better and calmer.

GROUP

2

Day
One

GROUP

2

1. HOW TO RECOGNIZE TENSION
   AND RELAXATION IN MUSCLES

Day One concentrates on the legs and on how to recognize tension and relaxation in the thigh muscles. Lie on the floor, legs slightly apart, arms by your side, head supported by a large firm pillow. A small pillow should be placed under each knee. Allow about 30 minutes for the session.

a. Breathe in and out regularly 10 times, and then gently feel the front of your right thigh with the middle finger of your right hand. (More detailed breathing techniques are taught on Day Two.) Keep this finger rigid and prod the thigh muscle. The sensation will be a bit like prodding a beach li-lo or well-filled hot water bottle. The thigh muscles are bound together around the thigh bone in a tight sheath, like the outside rubber on a hot water bottle or air bed, and when muscles are relaxed they feel wobbly, like the water in a hot water bottle. *Try to stay with this feeling* in the thigh muscle, though at first this will be difficult until the next manoeuvre (b) gives you a contrasting feeling.

b. Lift your right leg off the floor and hold it so that the right foot is just off the ground. Keep it there while you count five. First of all you will feel a sort of 'wormy' wriggling feeling in the calf and lower leg muscles. They are having *proprioceptive* problems and have difficulty in analyzing these as they don't quite know what you are expecting of them. This will give you your first positive experience of proprioceptive activity in a muscle group. More important now is to prod the front of the thigh once again. It will feel stony hard. *Stay with the feeling while you count slowly to 20.* Prod the muscle repeatedly to confirm the feeling from your prodding finger and the feelings coming from inside the muscle. *Count slowly to 20 again.* Now you will be feeling pressure in your *left* heel, *left* hip and *left* shoulder. Again proprioceptive messages will be coming to your brain from these areas. Perhaps they are signalling 'What shall we do? Is he trying to right himself?'

c. Now resume the starting (resting) position with the right leg on the floor. Breathe gently in and out 10 times and again prod the right thigh muscle, staying with the relaxed muscle feeling and thinking how different it feels from the tensed muscle.

24

a   Breathe in and out regularly 10 times. Prod right thigh muscle of right leg with rigid middle finger of right hand. Stay with the feeling in thigh muscle.

b   Lift right leg off floor. Hold for count of five. Prod thigh muscle again. Count slowly to 20, prodding muscle repeatedly and staying with tense feeling of muscle. Count slowly to 20 again.

GROUP

2

c   Resume starting position. Breathe in and out gently 10 times, and prod thigh muscle. Concentrate on how relaxed it feels.

Repeat this whole procedure three times with the right leg, and then repeat with the left leg. (Right-handed people usually learn to relax the right side of the body more easily than the left, and *vice versa*.)

2. ANTICIPATING TENSION AND RELAXATION

By now you will have started to learn the difference between tense and relaxed muscles and the proprioceptive impulses they generate. The final part of the first day's work involves the mobilization or recognition of other proprioceptive sensations that occur during muscle tension. You have already experienced these in the 'confused' muscles and joints described in Exercise 1 above. Now you must learn to anticipate the feel of these in the active muscle groups of the thigh that have been the object of your previous exercise.

a. First *concentrate* on how you *remember* the tense feeling of your thigh muscles. When you have an inkling of what this is then lift the leg slightly and put the muscle into tension. Try to match the two feelings.

b. Then, while the leg is still 'in tension' and before you replace it into the 'easy lie' position, try to remember the (pleasant) relaxed position. Again, when you have some recall of this, unstress the leg. Savour the relaxation.

c. Repeat for the other leg.

GROUP

2

Move on to Day Two when you are ready.

Note

Many people in Group 3 will be on medical treatment regimes, especially for blood pressure and heart conditions. It is essential that they let their prescribing physicians know that they are about to embark on a relaxation response type of training routine, not because there is any intrinsic danger in the method but because it might well be necessary to reduce the quantity of medicines and drugs taken daily once the relaxation response has been mastered. More information about how relaxation can help certain conditions will be found in Chapter 13.

Preliminaries

Although specially useful for the 60-plus age group and the disabled, many other people who find that tension is producing symptoms benefit from this simple system. It is based on the general principles of Swedish and Oriental self-massage, which teach recognition of essential sensations with the distinctive characteristics involved in the relaxation response. These arise from the skin and subcutaneous tissue rather than from muscles and joints, as in Group 2. (See Group 2, pages 22 to 23.)

First refer back to pages 12 to 14 for the basic relaxation response requirements. Most of these massage relaxation techniques can be learned in a sitting position. Some Oriental massages involving the upper limbs, face and trunk are traditionally carried out from the kneeling position. However, most people find kneeling uncomfortable, to start with at any rate; in which case, if discomfort is experienced, continue the exercises standing up.

Learn the bare bones of the massage relaxation technique until it is automatic before attempting to synchronize any breathing and feeling response (see Days Two and Three). Allow about 30 minutes for the session.

GROUP

1. HANDS (SWEDISH REGIME)

a. Take the left hand, with its palm upwards, and hold it in the right hand so that the right thumb can rub (massage) the palm of the left hand, and the thumb and fingers. Get an idea of gentle massage in contrast to harder friction.

b. Turn the left hand over and give friction (fast massage) to the back of the left hand, using the right thumb. While giving friction concentrate on breathing *in*, counting one – and – two – and – three – and.

Repeat with other hand.

GROUP

3

c. Now rest your left hand on your knee (palm towards the leg), hand slightly clasped. Use palm of right hand to stroke from your fingers towards the wrist of your left hand. Start with quite firm stroking and gradually make stroking lighter as you move up the hand. By the time the finger bases are reached the stroking should be light. While you are thus stroking (massaging), concentrate on the *out* breathing process of one – and – two – and – three – and. Repeat with other hand.

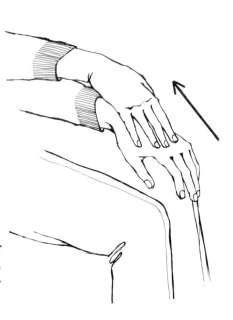

Repeat the Swedish regime for 15 minutes.

2. HANDS (ORIENTAL REGIME)

This Oriental massage is done in a kneeling position, and to do it properly you need a watch with a minute hand.

1. Hand rub

a. Place hands together in the 'prayer' position with thumbs at nose level. Rub together vigorously and quite firmly for a full one minute. This seems like a long time and gives the experience of quite severe tension and stress in the arms and hands. Keep with this feeling and commit it to your memory.

b. After the minute is up, shake the hands as if you were shaking off some washing-up water. Shake for one full minute, first using the whole arm and then both hands only. The tension release is felt during this process. Keep with this feeling and try to remember it.

c. Then, using the back of the right hand, friction the back of the left hand quite firmly, recalling the feeling of tension. Do this 10 times.

d. Then slide all five fingers of the right hand lightly down over the five fingers of the left hand, remembering, if you can, the relaxed feeling you got after your prayer hand rub and shake.

Repeat the friction and stroking 10 times.

29

2. Rotating fingers

Place the left hand in your lap and, in turn, take each finger and thumb gently by the thumb and forefinger of the right hand and rotate it, breathing *in* one – and – two – and – three – and – as you rotate each finger, and breathing *out* as you move to the next finger. Repeat with the other hand.

3. Pinching down at webs

Place the left hand in your lap and with the finger and thumb of the right hand pinch down at the webs between the fingers quite firmly. Breathe *out* one – and – two – and – three – and – as you do so. Repeat five times, then repeat with the other hand.

4. Finger squeeze

a. Enclose, in turn, the thumb and fingers of the left hand in the clenched right hand. Squeeze hard and gently pull (not with arthritic hands). Repeat until each finger of the left hand has had its squeeze, and keep with the feeling of tension in the active right hand as you do so.

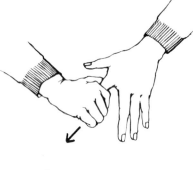

b. Then put both hands together in the 'prayer' position and rub vigorously for 30 seconds, again keeping with the feeling of tension now in both arms.

c. Shake the tension out again and reinforce the memory of relaxation as you do so.

Move on to Day Two when you are ready.

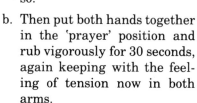

Essential breathing technique

Preliminaries

All groups participate in the same training regime on Day Two, so fundamental is this breathing technique to learning how to relax. Groups 1 and 2 usually learn this breathing technique best in a lying position, while Group 3 often finds that a sitting position is easier.

Before teaching the breathing technique, I first get novices to learn what a four-second breath feels like. It is a four-second breath in, and a four-second breath out. This must be practised a few times by the clock until memory makes it automatic. The timing is important because it is the basis of all subsequent breathing techniques.

Most people have confused ideas about deep breathing and equate it with chest expansion and effort. In fact, deep and rapid breathing is known to generate tension and may provide unpleasant panic attacks. The type of breathing necessary for the relaxation response is nothing like this. Already on Day One you will have started to get an idea of relaxation response breathing. But, as Day One concentrated mostly on muscle control, a very simple approximation of the ideal breathing technique was accepted as second best, and was certainly better than the normal type of shallow and irregular breathing that we use every day.

Note

Breathing exercises as well as all the other exercises should not be carried out within two hours of a substantial meal.

GROUP

1

GROUP

2

GROUP

3

Day Two

GROUP

1

GROUP

2

GROUP

3

1. LEARNING THE TECHNIQUE OF RELAXED BREATHING

1. Relaxed muscles

First take up your relaxation training position and work your way into feeling your muscles relax. Group 2 learnt how to do this on Day One, and I repeat the basic technique here. Lie on the floor, legs slightly apart, arms by your side, head supported by a large firm pillow. A small pillow should be placed under each knee.

a. Breathe in and out regularly 10 times, and then gently feel the front of your right thigh with the middle finger of your right hand. Keep this finger rigid and prod the thigh muscle. The sensation will be a bit like prodding a beach li-lo or well-filled hot water bottle. The thigh muscles are bound together around the thigh bone in a tight sheath, like the outside rubber on a hot water bottle or air bed; when muscles are relaxed they feel wobbly, like the water in a hot water bottle. Try to stay with this feeling in the thigh muscle, though at first this will be difficult until the next manoeuvre (b) gives you a contrasting feeling.

b. To recognize tension in the muscles of the leg, lift your right leg off the floor and hold it so that the right foot is just off the ground. Keep it there while you count five. First of all you will feel a sort of 'wormy' wriggling feeling in the calf and lower leg muscles. Prod the front of the thigh once again. It will feel stony hard. Stay with this feeling while you count slowly to 20. Prod the muscle repeatedly to confirm the feeling from your prodding finger and the feelings coming from inside the muscle. Count slowly to 20 again. Now you will be feeling pressure in your left heel, left hip and left shoulder.

c. Now resume the starting (resting) position with the right leg on the floor. Breathe gently in and out and again prod the right thigh muscle, staying with the relaxed muscle feeling and thinking how different it feels from the tensed muscle.

Repeat with the left leg. (Right-handed people usually learn to relax the right side of the body more easily than the left, and *vice versa*.)

32

a   Breathe in and out regularly 10 times. Prod right thigh muscle of right leg with rigid middle finger of right hand. Stay with the feeling in thigh muscle.

b   Lift right leg off floor. Hold for count of five. Prod thigh muscle again. Count slowly to 20, prodding muscle repeatedly and staying with tense feeling of muscle. Count slowly to 20 again.

c   Resume starting position. Breathe in and out gently 10 times, and prod thigh muscle. Concentrate on how relaxed it feels.

GROUP 1

GROUP 2

GROUP 3

2. Smooth breathing

Once your muscles are relaxed try to stay with this feeling while taking a few four-second breaths in and out. (The four-second breath started as the one – and – two – and – three – and breathing technique that Groups 1 and 3 used on Day One.) Here I want you all to concentrate on the *smoothness* of your breathing and to lose the one – and – two – and – three – and count.

Day
Two

GROUP

1

GROUP

2

GROUP

3

3. Quiet breathing

To start with your breaths in and out will sound quite different to each other. Breathing *in* is usually noisier than breathing *out*. This must be corrected and it may need a fair amount of concentration and practice to do this. When breathing *in* quietens, breathing immediately feels better; it loses its gasping in-rush of air characteristic. Model the breathing-*in* sound on the breathing-*out* sound. As mentioned before, to begin you will need a watch with a second-hand to check that your four-second timing is accurate.

4. Pendulum breathing

Once you have mastered the timing and the sound, the next thing is to concentrate on losing the pauses at full inspiration and at full expiration. Try to imagine a large pendulum in a clock. As the pendulum reaches the full sweep at one side of its swing it stops momentarily before swinging back. You can't actually see it stop of course, but this momentary pause is exactly the pause you are trying to build into your relaxation breathing. We will call this breathing technique pendulum breathing.

At first the same-sound breathing and the constant swish of air through the chest seems highly unnatural. Really it is very natural, but you are not yet used to it. Once the four-second, constant intensity, almost continuous air exchange is learned you are well on the way to mastering the breathing side of the relaxation technique, and your body will start to respond to this.

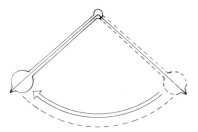

Four-second breath *in*.

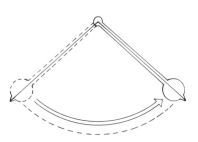

Four-second breath *out*.

34

2. BREATHING PRACTICE

Persevere with this new breathing technique for 15 minutes at a time. Your aim is to stop the exercise naturally after 15 minutes but at first you will be wildly inaccurate as to how long you have been practising. Four to five minutes seem like 15. In the early days you will need a watch or timer to check your timing. When you naturally and gently stop your relaxation breathing at around 15 minutes you will be well on the way to success.

After the pendulum breathing session is over, try to give yourself a few minutes to adjust before carrying on with any activity.

Concentrating on this unusual type of breathing allows you to learn to dismiss the everyday thoughts that can intrude on most relaxation programmes at the beginning. Almost always at first however, these thoughts will tend to intrude and it is necessary to turn away from them. Sometimes a mantra is helpful when this happens (see page 13).

To begin, practise this breathing programme with your eyes closed. As it becomes more automatic the eyes can be opened and the process continued. Many people find that things around them look different after 10 to 15 minutes of relaxation breathing. They unexpectedly appear new or unusual.

Some people, when they start these very important breathing exercises, notice that their internal body sounds rather intrusive. Noises of the heart beat, 'swishing' experiences in the head or a fluttering in the throat and chest are common too. They pass off as you get used to the new technique.

Exactly what happens during the relaxed pendulum breathing is very complex. The amount of oxygen that the body uses is considerably decreased compared with the normal resting state, and the body enters a changed state of functioning. A very simple physiological change takes place which makes you feel rested and revitalized.

Note

Groups 2 and 3 will find that mastering the relaxation breathing technique will be sufficient to occupy them on Day Two. In fact, until the controlled and regular pendulum breathing becomes acceptable and understood it is probably not worthwhile moving on to Day Three regimes. Group 1, however, is an energetic and forward-pressing group and can usually add a further element of yoga to the second day.

Groups 2 and 3 may be interested in using the Group 1 *Aeroplane* exercises (pages 36 to 37) as a warm-up before starting their daily programme.

GROUP

1

GROUP

2

GROUP

3

GROUP

1

Yoga component

AEROPLANE (1)

This exercise introduces arm movements. First practise the mechanics of the exercise, and then add the one – and – two – and – three – pause – breathing timing to movements.

a. Stand with legs apart (up to 3 feet/1 metre).

b. Raise the arms so that they are at right angles to the body (in the child's aeroplane position). As arms are raised to aeroplane position gradually turn right foot out so that it moves through a right angle; at the same time rotate the left foot slightly into a 'pigeon toed' position.

c. Lower arms to body and restore feet to normal position. Repeat arm raising, but this time turn left foot out and right foot in.

Synchronization: Now introduce breathing sequence one – and – two – and – three – pause – to each foot/arm manoeuvre. Repeat three to five times.

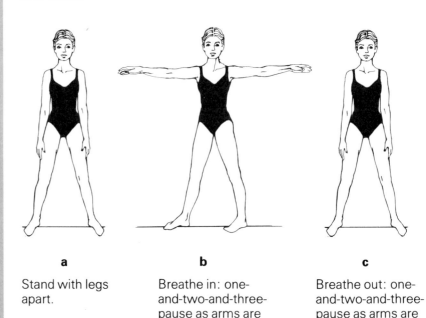

a	b	c
Stand with legs apart.	Breathe in: one-and-two-and-three-pause as arms are raised and feet rotate.	Breathe out: one-and-two-and-three-pause as arms are lowered and feet restored to starting position.

36

AEROPLANE (2)

This is an extension of (1). Again learn the mechanics of the movement before attempting breath synchronization. Often considerable creaking of joints will be heard, even in young people, during this simple exercise. The arms should be in the aeroplane position throughout.

a. The arms are raised to the aeroplane position.

b. Bend the trunk sideways at the hips, bringing the right hand down towards the right foot.

c. Then return the body to its upright position, arms parallel to the floor, and bend to the other side.

Synchronization: The first one – and – two – and – three – pause – breath in is done on the sideways bend down, and the breath is let out on the upward movement.

   Repeat until gently tired.

GROUP

1

a
Raise arms to
aeroplane position.

b
Breathe in: one-
and-two-and-three-
pause as you bend
down.

c
Breathe out: one-
and-two-and-three-
pause as you
straighten and
breathe in as you
bend to left.

ALL GROUPS

GROUP

1

Revision and Synchronization

This is a day for revising the techniques learned on Days One and Two, and for blending the relaxation breathing technique to the more mechanical processes learned on Day One.

Group 1: try to give yourselves at least 30 minutes' revision training, twice a day.

Yoga component

1. STAND, STRETCH AND BREATHE

Start as described on page 18 and carry out the *Stand, stretch and breathe* (get taller) exercise, synchronizing with the breathing technique mastered on Day Two. Do this five times. It will seem more difficult to 'get tall' because the controlled breathing that you have now learned is not so much of a puff and blow as was the so-called deep breathing practised on Day One. Already you see how the course changes as it proceeds, and you will feel yourself changing with it.

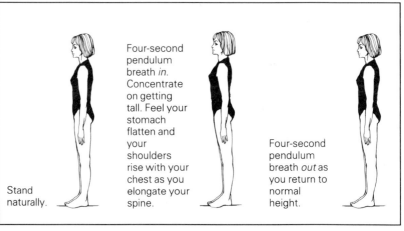

Stand naturally.

Four-second pendulum breath *in*. Concentrate on getting tall. Feel your stomach flatten and your shoulders rise with your chest as you elongate your spine.

Four-second pendulum breath *out* as you return to normal height.

2. LEG BALANCE AND BREATHE

Change to the *Leg balance and breathe* exercise (right and left leg raising exercises), again five times for each leg using pendulum breathing.

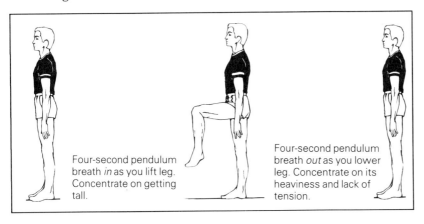

Four-second pendulum breath *in* as you lift leg. Concentrate on getting tall.

Four-second pendulum breath *out* as you lower leg. Concentrate on its heaviness and lack of tension.

3. AEROPLANE (1)

Now add the *Aeroplane (1)* exercise, the yoga component from Day Two. This will seem quite difficult to start with and synchronization with the relaxation-type breathing will usually pose problems. If you have great difficulty, then sit down and practise the four-second in four-second out, same noise, clock-pendulum breathing for five minutes. Then, when you have this under control, stand up and do the *Aeroplane (1)* foot twist 10 times until you get a semblance of grace and rhythm into the exercise.

Concentrate on the tension felt in the arms raised/twisted leg position at the end of the four-second breathing-in part of the exercise, and then compare it with the relative relaxation felt when standing straight during the breath-out element.

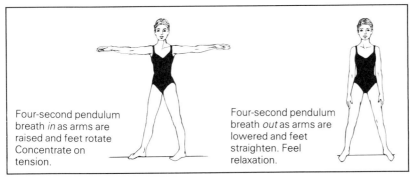

Four-second pendulum breath *in* as arms are raised and feet rotate Concentrate on tension.

Four-second pendulum breath *out* as arms are lowered and feet straighten. Feel relaxation.

GROUP

1

4. AEROPLANE (2)

Finally move on to *Aeroplane (2)*. Starting in the aeroplane position the right hand and arm slowly sweeps down towards the right ankle, and as it does so the left arm moves upwards. Both arms are still in time as the right hand reaches the right ankle and toes. Synchronization of the four-second breathing is difficult to start with. Breathe in as you bend down; breathe out as you return to the aeroplane position, and breathe in again as the left hand slowly plunges down from the aeroplane position, making for the left ankle and toes and arriving there four seconds later. Repeat four or five times.

During four-second pendulum breath *in*, bend over towards ankle.

During four-second pendulum breath *out*, straighten, then breathe in as you bend to other side.

What you are doing

There is nothing related to magic in these exercises. All they do is slowly teach a discipline of relaxation through breathing and movement. They condition the body to stop thinking while the new relaxation type breathing is being accepted by the mind and body.

Autogenic component

Repeat the Day One procedure (page 21). The mantra component is entirely variable and optional. On Day One I suggested 'I am relaxed and at peace with myself.' It can just as easily be 'Holy Mary, Mother of God' or 'Gentle Jesus meek and mild', or a suitable short but intrinsically powerful repeated phrase from a Vedic scripture. The purpose of the mantra is to learn a technique of redirecting the thoughts *away* from problem-solving or intrusive day dreams. It really says, 'I dismiss everyday problems – I am at peace with myself.' (See also Chapter 3.)

40

The whole relaxation experience of Day Three should last about half an hour, and be followed by a gentle 'get up and go' routine. If you like, start each day with the *Aeroplane* exercises (pages 36 and 37) as a warm-up.

1. MUSCLE RELAXATION

Reread what is written on pages 22 and 23 on muscle relaxation.

2. HOW TO RECOGNIZE RELAXATION

Restart Day One routine, but this time breathe in and out in the four-second clock-pendulum way detailed in Day Two. After Routine a is blended to the relaxation response breathing, introduce Routine b.

You will have difficulty in synchronizing your newly learned breathing with your exercises and you may find yourself slipping back into ordinary or 'deep' breathing as you do so. Expect this and correct yourself.

Some people find this process easier to master if they record Day One, Routine b into a tape recorder, quite slowly, and then play it back while they are blending it with the pendulum breathing technique.

Instead of counting to 20, make an unconscious and private deal with yourself to do five (20-second) right leg raises and then five (20-second) left leg raises followed by an equal time of 'both legs rest' experience.

GROUP

Take 10 four-second pendulum breaths in and out, then gently feel front of right thigh with middle finger of right hand. Then prod thigh muscle with rigid finger, and continue with pendulum breathing. Your leg should feel relaxed.

Lift right leg off floor. Hold for 20 seconds (without counting), and prod front of thigh. Keep with pendulum breathing. Repeat with left leg, then rest and feel the relaxation.

GROUP

2

3. ANTICIPATING TENSION AND RELAXATION

Concentrate on experiencing the tension feeling without actually raising the leg. If you cannot remember, then raise the leg and the memory will flood back. While the leg is tense compare it with the feeling in the other (relaxed) leg. While still enjoying your four-second pendulum breaths, remember the total leg relaxation feeling. Then invite this memory back while actually relaxing the leg. *The closer you get to remembering the relaxed feeling, the nearer you are to mastering the relaxation response.*

4. GET UP AND GO

Follow your relaxation with a gentle get up and go routine. Indulge in a few good stretches to make yourself feel alert and refreshed.

Preliminaries

There was much more learning on Day One than on Day Two, so run through page 27 and then relearn the Swedish regime and the Oriental. The session should take about 30 minutes.

If you want to start with a warm-up exercise, do *Aeroplane (1)* and *(2)* on pages 36 and 37. They can be carried out each day before other relaxation techniques.

1. HANDS (SWEDISH REGIME)

a. Massage each hand in turn for five periods of four-second pendulum breathing (one breath for each finger and the thumb). *Concentrate* on the feeling of softness and relaxation that this produces.

b. Turn the hand over and give friction to each finger – as many times as you can on each digit during a four-second in four-second out pendulum breath.

Then place both hands in your lap. Which one feels more relaxed? The right one will feel more relaxed, but the left will also feel a bit more relaxed than it did to start with. Stay with this relaxed feeling and try to remember it. Then try to remember what your right hand felt like when it was in action, first giving the massage and then the friction. Reinforce this feeling by giving your left hand another friction with your right hand. Rest again and concentrate on the pendulum breathing and the relaxed feeling in the hands.

c. Now move on to Routine c, again in tune with the four-second in and out pendulum breathing. The left hand becomes very relaxed during this procedure. After 10 pendulum sequences allow both hands to remain still on the thighs. Stay with this relaxed feeling.

GROUP

3

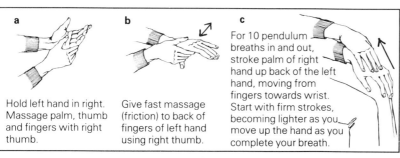

a Hold left hand in right. Massage palm, thumb and fingers with right thumb.

b Give fast massage (friction) to back of fingers of left hand using right thumb.

c For 10 pendulum breaths in and out, stroke palm of right hand up back of the left hand, moving from fingers towards wrist. Start with firm strokes, becoming lighter as you move up the hand as you complete your breath.

Day Three

GROUP
3

2. HANDS (ORIENTAL REGIME)

1. *Hand rub*

a. This time start by carrying out the prayer hand rub for 10 to 12 in and out pendulum breaths. The tension associated with this builds up as the exercise proceeds.

b. Shake out the tension and concentrate on remembering this feeling of lack of tension (relaxation).

c. Then again experience tension in the right hand by administering a friction by the back of the right hand to the back of the left hand for 10 to 12 pendulum breaths.

d. Then using five fingers of the right hand slide these over the five fingers of the left hand and enjoy the relaxed feeling that develops.

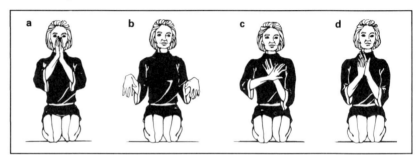

Next carry out the remaining hand exercises learned on Day One. All the time concentrate on the relaxation response breathing and the feeling of relaxation that follows the massage and friction.

2. *Rotating fingers*

Using the thumb and forefinger of your right hand, gently rotate a left-hand finger during a pendulum breath *in*. Repeat with other fingers and thumb of left hand, then repeat with other hand.

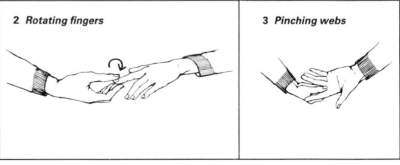

2 *Rotating fingers*

3 *Pinching webs*

3. *Pinching down at webs*

Quite firmly, with the finger and thumb of your right hand, pinch down at a web between the fingers of your left hand during a pendulum breath out. Pinch down at each web in turn and repeat five times. Repeat with other hand.

4. *Finger squeeze*

a. In turn, squeeze each finger of the left hand hard in your clenched right hand, then gently pull (not for arthritic hands). Keep with the feeling of tension in the active right hand as you do so.

b. Then put both hands together in the prayer position and rub vigorously for 30 seconds. Feel the tension.

c. Shake the tension out of your arms. Feel the relaxation.

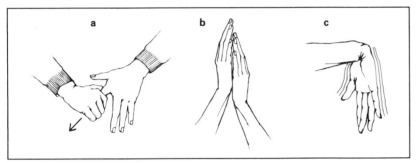

What you are doing

You are reinforcing the relaxation response by pendulum type four-second in/four-second out breathing while carrying out mild stress and relaxation exercises. *If done conscientiously for half an hour per day you will be able to gain the first insights into the value of the relaxation breathing response and will be ready for the introduction of new relaxation facilitating experiences on Day Four.*

Move on to Day Four when you are ready.

GROUP

Day Four

GROUP

1

Yoga component

The following simple yoga exercises are carried out in such a way that each manoeuvre can be matched to a four-second controlled breath.

1. SIT AND STRETCH

a. Sit on the floor with your back resting against the wall.

b. As you start your four-second breath in, reach forward with your arms and grasp your toes or ankles as you come to full inspiration (pendulum).

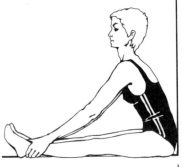

c. Then pause to allow your head to fall into the space between your legs.

d. As the pendulum starts to move again, gradually reverse the exercise so that when your breath-out is completed you have reached the sitting position again.

Repeat five to 10 times.

46

2. PRESS-UPS

a. This is a press-up type of yoga exercise. Lie on your tummy, with your forehead on the floor and hands beneath shoulders.

b. Very slowly, tilt head back, push hands against floor and press up to reach the full up position as the four-second breath in reaches the pendulum pause. The head should be pulled back as far as possible. (A girl with long hair will feel her hair slapping into her back.)

c. Then with the four-second expiration smoothly return to the flat on-the-floor position at the end of the expiration phase.

Repeat five to 10 times.

GROUP

1

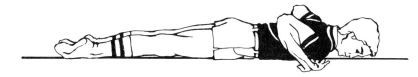

a Lie on stomach in press-up position with hands beneath shoulders.

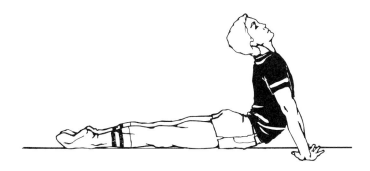

b Start four-second pendulum breath in and reach full up position at full inspiration. Head back.

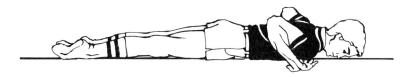

c As you pendulum breathe out, return to flat-on-the-floor by end of expiration.

Day Four

GROUP 1

3. CHEST TWIST

a. Sit in the middle of the room with the legs outstretched.

b. Start the four-second breathe in. Place right foot over left thigh, place right hand behind you and bring left hand to hold left knee.

c. Slowly twist to right as far as possible, and turning your head towards your back. Pull in at the waist, stretching the trunk tall. By now you will ideally have reached the four-second pendulum breath position of full inspiration.

d. Return to the sitting up straight position during four-second exhalation. Then repeat in the opposite direction.

This exercise is quite difficult and may well have to be practised a few times so that the mechanics can be mastered before they are synchronized with the breathing.

a Sit in middle of room, legs outstretched.

b During four-second pendulum breath in, place right foot over left leg, then place right hand behind you and hold left knee with left hand.

c Slowly twist to right as far as possible. Stretch body and turn head as far as it will go.

48

Autogenic component

On Day Four another autogenic component is added: the experience of warmth. Take up a comfortable reclining position, which will feel restful after the vigorous yoga. This should, if possible, be in a 'safe' place, away from interruptions and telephones. You really need 20 minutes of peace in order to work on this autogenic system.

a. Start concentrating on your right arm, saying to yourself, 'My arm feels warm – my arm feels warm.' You cannot control or force this feeling. It has to come as part and parcel of a feeling of relaxation. Again the controlled pendulum breathing helps. It may not be possible to experience this warm feeling to start with, in which case after spending a few minutes on it without effect abandon the process until the next day, going back to Day One autogenics. Some students of autogenics find that this experience of warmth needs several days' practice before it comes. Once it occurs leave it and concentrate on the left arm, again expecting the warm feeling. A passive receptive state, with well-synchronized pendulum breathing and the autogenic mantra, usually works in the end.

b. Once warmth can be experienced in this way in the upper limbs, extend it to the neck and face. About 20 minutes, twice daily, is an adequate warmth experience training session.

GROUP

1

Day Four

GROUP

2

Preliminaries

Having synchronized leg relaxation with pendulum type breathing on Day Three, the next component to be added is arm relaxation. Start by sitting in a chair, and allow yourself 10 minutes for each of the three stages of arm and hand relaxation. Warm up with the *Aeroplane* exercises first if you like (see pages 36 and 37).

1. HAND RELAXATION

a. After about 10 breaths of pendulum breathing the 'I'm relaxing better' feeling will flood in. Once this is experienced concentrate your thoughts on your left hand (if you are right-handed; your right if you are left-handed).

b. Tension in the hands is not as easy to assess as leg tension because the fingers are feeling tenseness generated elsewhere in the arm. A good way to assess hand and finger tension is to place a stiff postcard between the fingers of the left hand and try to hold it there while the right hand tries gently to pull it free. The sort of feeling of tension experienced is very much what the victim of writer's cramp feels as he tries to speed his pen across the page in anticipation of his thoughts or to some real or imagined deadline. As the hand muscles relax (as they will easily do as the pendulum breathing proceeds), the postcard will slip easily through the fingers, even though they remain quite close together. Once the left hand has learnt the feeling of relaxation, the right hand can be taught to experience the same thing.

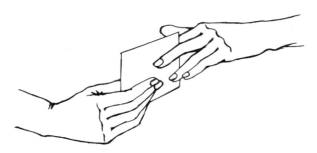

c. Then concentrate on the relaxed left hand, giving the right fleeting attention until it too relaxes.

50

By now you will be beginning to master an art that you are going to use a lot in the future – the art of learning to relax a tense part of the body quickly, by developing an awareness of tension versus relaxation. You are learning to be aware of the feeling of relaxation, and learning to be able to stay with this feeling in conjunction with your pendulum breathing. You will be able to spot tension without having to make yourself *experience* it. On Day One you had to feel the hardness of your leg muscles to experience tension in a positive way. Now you have to recognize and remember the tense feeling without making that part of the body tense by contracting muscles.

d. *Deep hand relaxation:* Start with the muscles in the hand. Remember the relaxed feeling and then reinforce the relaxation feeling without actually having to test that you have relaxed the particular muscles. It sounds complicated but it is really quite easy. Practise deep hand relaxation by allowing the hand to spread out and feel big. A good tip is to write down your name and address a few times and then progressively get that hand to relax. Quite soon the pen refuses to mark the paper as the muscle tension drains away. Once you have the feel of this, stay with this feeling for 10 to 20 pendulum breaths.

2. LOWER ARM RELAXATION

GROUP 2

Next direct your attention to the forearm muscles, starting again with the left arm. You probably will not need to remind yourself how the tense muscles on either side of the forearm feel; and, in any case, you should not try to build a 'tension test' into your regime. A good way to relax forearm muscles is as follows.

a. Lie down in your relaxation room. After a few pendulum breaths rest the elbows on the floor and raise forearms and hands upwards towards the ceiling. Then let hands 'gravity flop' at the wrists. Repeat this five times.

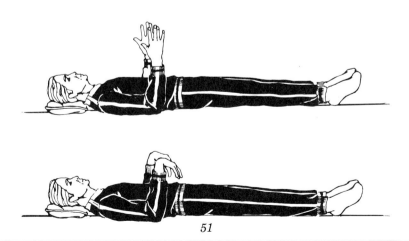

GROUP

2

b. Then, using the right hand (we are again dealing with right-handed people), feel the degree of relaxation at the wrist by lifting the left wrist and letting it fall back again. Stay with this hand and lower arm relaxation feeling.

c. Transfer your attention to the right hand. Immediately you will note that the right wrist and arm will be much more difficult to relax after a gravity flop exercise than the left. Practise the right arm and hand gravity flop several times until you can get them to become as relaxed as the left. This may need 10 or 20 flops, all practised alongside pendulum breathing. Eventually some semblance of equal relaxation will be learned. Stay with this feeling.

d. Repeat gravity flops, using both arms. Check for equal relaxation.

3. UPPER ARM RELAXATION

This is carried out in a sitting position. With the upper arm, concentrate on producing a relaxed biceps muscle. This muscle rests on the inner sides of the upper arm and is opposed by the triceps muscle behind the arm. Usually when the biceps is relaxed the triceps is in contraction and is tense. It is difficult to experience the feeling of a tense triceps, and the big arm-lifting muscle called the deltoid muscle, unless one arm holds the other and attempts to move it away from the body. Doing this, however, tends to teach tension rather than relaxation in muscle groups.

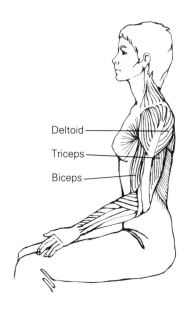

Deltoid —
Triceps —
Biceps —

a. To relax the upper arm, start by feeling the 'super-wobbly' left biceps moving between your right hand fingers as you gently shake the tension out of it. Stay with the feeling as you actively relax those triceps muscles. As they relax you will feel the biceps go hard and tight again. This is only natural, for these muscles work in antagonism. Gradually, however, you will be able to work through these feelings and get the whole arm to feel relaxed.

Feel your left biceps move as you shake tension out of it with fingers of right hand. Stay with this feeling as you relax the triceps muscle.

4. PENDULUM BREATHING

When your self-teaching session is over, stay with your relaxed arm feelings for five to 10 minutes, pendulum breathing throughout.

GROUP

2

53

Day Four

1. ARM RELAXATION

a. Sit with your left arm supported by a pillow in your lap. Knead and wobble the big muscles of your left upper arm with the whole of your right hand, making large circular movements. At the same time practise your pendulum breathing.

b. After five minutes or so, give this same area a fingertip friction, as fast as you like for one minute. Then repeat the kneading. A more relaxed feeling will occur in the upper arm.

c. Move down to the forearm and do the same with this, and finally move down to the left hand. Stay with the relaxed feeling in the arm and enjoy its first taste of relaxation perhaps for years, keeping the breathing nice and regular. This will take about 15 minutes.

d. Now direct your attention to the right arm, using your recently relaxed left hand as the masseur. Right-handed people will have more trouble relaxing the right side of the body, and so we always start relaxation training with the opposite, easier to relax, side of the body.

GROUP

2. MORE HAND AND ARM RELAXATION

Read the section for Group 2 on Day Four (pages 52 to 53). Follow through these three stages of hand and arm relaxation if you are not too tired. The two experiences are complementary and helpful to most people.

54

Revision and Synchronization

The idea today is to put together a relaxation programme. This will not be your final programme – that comes later as a few more elements are built into the system. The aim at this half-way stage is to use your half hour (hopefully twice a day) in an economical but fruitful way by making the techniques automatic and concentrating on making the difficult parts less difficult. As you learn the various techniques you will find that you enjoy, and are more preoccupied with, the already pleasurable and *positive* parts of the programme. It is through these *positive* feelings that success in relaxation is ultimately attained.

ALL GROUPS

Yoga revision

GROUP 1

1. PENDULUM BREATHING

Put together your yoga programme against the background of pendulum breathing (learned on Day Two). Get into the swing of this with five pendulum breathing cycles to start your session.

2. STAND, STRETCH AND BREATHE

Practise *Stand, stretch and breathe* for 10 breaths (synchronized with pendulum breathing as on Day Three).

3. LEG BALANCE AND BREATHE

Practise *Leg balance and breathe* for 10 breaths, each leg (synchronized with pendulum breathing as on Day Three).

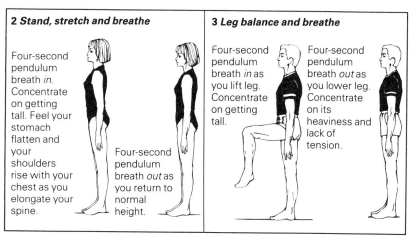

2 Stand, stretch and breathe

Four-second pendulum breath *in*. Concentrate on getting tall. Feel your stomach flatten and your shoulders rise with your chest as you elongate your spine.

Four-second pendulum breath *out* as you return to normal height.

3 Leg balance and breathe

Four-second pendulum breath *in* as you lift leg. Concentrate on getting tall.

Four-second pendulum breath *out* as you lower leg. Concentrate on its heaviness and lack of tension.

GROUP

1

4. AEROPLANE

Practise *Aeroplane 1 and 2* for 10 breaths, right and left, each exercise (synchronized with pendulum breathing as on Day Three).

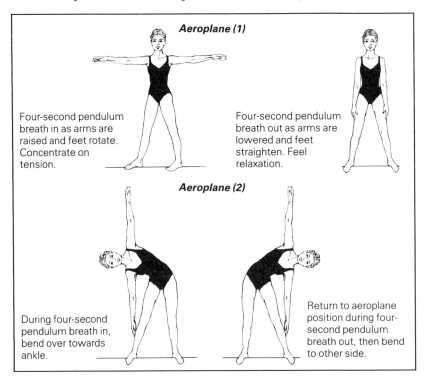

Aeroplane (1)

Four-second pendulum breath in as arms are raised and feet rotate. Concentrate on tension.

Four-second pendulum breath out as arms are lowered and feet straighten. Feel relaxation.

Aeroplane (2)

During four-second pendulum breath in, bend over towards ankle.

Return to aeroplane position during four-second pendulum breath out, then bend to other side.

5. SIT AND STRETCH

Practise *Sit and stretch* five times (Day Four).

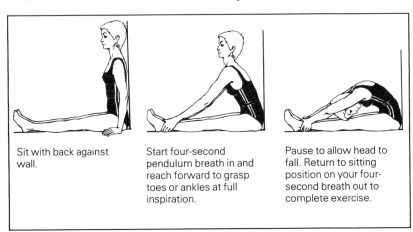

Sit with back against wall.

Start four-second pendulum breath in and reach forward to grasp toes or ankles at full inspiration.

Pause to allow head to fall. Return to sitting position on your four-second breath out to complete exercise.

6. PRESS-UPS

Practise *Press-ups* five times (Day Four).

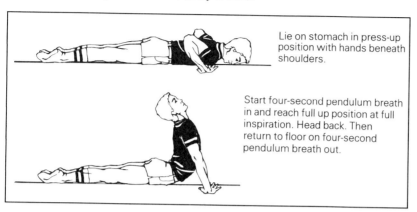

Lie on stomach in press-up position with hands beneath shoulders.

Start four-second pendulum breath in and reach full up position at full inspiration. Head back. Then return to floor on four-second pendulum breath out.

GROUP

1

7. CHEST TWIST

Practise *Chest twist* five times in each direction (Day Four).

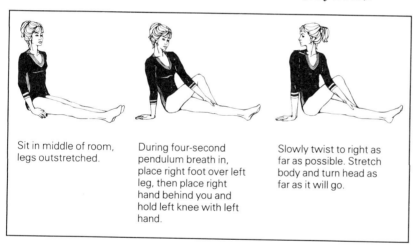

Sit in middle of room, legs outstretched.

During four-second pendulum breath in, place right foot over left leg, then place right hand behind you and hold left knee with left hand.

Slowly twist to right as far as possible. Stretch body and turn head as far as it will go.

Autogenic revision

1. Practise autogenic relaxation with mantra (Day One).
2. Practise autogenic warmth relaxation (Day Four).

Total time about 30 minutes

Day Five

GROUP 2

1. MUSCLE RELAXATION

Reread *Muscle relaxation* (Day One) and concentrate on the relationship of the relaxed muscle to the relaxed self. Reflect on the concepts of *proprium* and the relaxed muscle state.

2. PENDULUM BREATHING

Establish *Pendulum breathing* (Day Two) for 10 breaths, then carry out Day One *How to recognize tension and relaxation in muscles*, Routines a and b, while maintaining pendulum breathing.

3. FEELING THE RELAXED MUSCLE

Repeat Day One *How to recognize tension and relaxation in muscles*, Routine a only. (You are trying to forget muscle tension analysis; you must now only recognize the memory of it so that you can reject it.)

Take 10 four-second pendulum breaths in and out, then gently feel front of right thigh with middle finger of right hand. Then prod thigh muscle with rigid finger, and continue with pendulum breathing.

4. ARM RELAXATION

Carry out right and left hand, forearm and upper arm relaxation exercises (Day Four), concentrating on the positive relaxation principles.

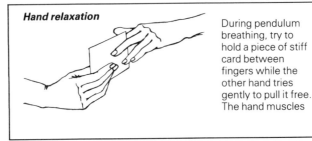

Hand relaxation

During pendulum breathing, try to hold a piece of stiff card between fingers while the other hand tries gently to pull it free. The hand muscles will relax. Then experience deep hand relaxation.

58

Forearm relaxation

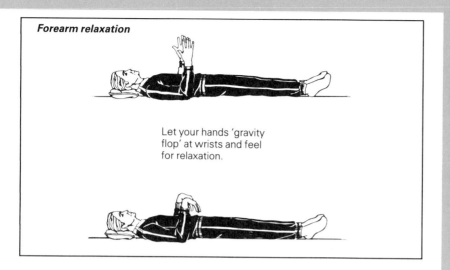

Let your hands 'gravity flop' at wrists and feel for relaxation.

Upper arm relaxation

Feel your left biceps move as you shake tension out of it with fingers of right hand. Stay with this feeling as you relax the triceps muscle.

Total time 30 minutes

GROUP

2

Day Five

Reorganize your self-massage and friction regimes into the following combined and logical format.

1. PENDULUM BREATHING

Practise pendulum breathing (Day Two) for five minutes.

2. ARM RELAXATION

Start your massage and friction exercises with the Day Four routines which are still fresh in your mind. (Five minutes)

While pendulum breathing, knead and wobble big muscles of left arm with whole of right hand, making large circular movements.

Then give fast fingertip friction to the same area and repeat on left forearm and hand.

Next relax the right arm.

3. SWEDISH AND ORIENTAL MASSAGE

Next practise the *Swedish regime* and *Oriental regime* from Day One. (Five minutes)

4. PENDULUM BREATHING

Practise pendulum breathing (Day Two) for five minutes.

5. AUTOGENIC RELAXATION

Read *Autogenic component* (Day One, Group 1), and while practising pendulum breathing carry out autogenic relaxation until you have completed the half hour programme.

GROUP

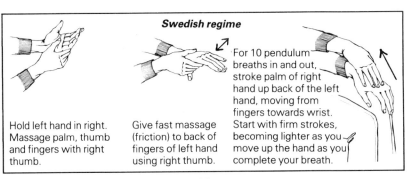

Swedish regime

Hold left hand in right. Massage palm, thumb and fingers with right thumb.

Give fast massage (friction) to back of fingers of left hand using right thumb.

For 10 pendulum breaths in and out, stroke palm of right hand up back of the left hand, moving from fingers towards wrist. Start with firm strokes, becoming lighter as you move up the hand as you complete your breath.

Oriental regime

Rub hands together vigorously and quite firmly to experience tension.

Shake hands to release tension.

Using back of right hand, friction the back of left hand quite firmly, recalling feeling of tension.

Slide fingers of right hand down over fingers of left, remembering and reinforcing the relaxed feeling felt after the hand rub.

Rotate the fingers and thumb of your left hand gently by thumb and forefinger of right hand during pendulum breath in and out.

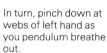

In turn, pinch down at webs of left hand as you pendulum breathe out.

Squeeze each finger of left hand hard, and gently pull as you pendulum breathe out. Rub hands in prayer position to feel tension then shake out tension and feel the relaxation.

Total time 30 minutes

GROUP

3

Day Six

GROUP

1

Yoga component

A little over half-way through the course, the yoga component introduces what are known as *poses* rather than exercises. Once the relaxation response can be achieved easily, it is possible to use a pose to switch off tension quickly – at home, in the office, or before a sports activity. I know a girl late into childbirth who used the yoga pose *Bhadra* to relax when she felt exhausted. And I once discovered a young man 'in *Bhadra*' at a medical exhibition; he found it refreshed him and revitalized his interest.

Here I recommend two classic poses – *Bhadrasana* and *Virasana*. A more athletic pose – *Sarvangasana* – may be practised as an optional extra by those athletic enough to enjoy it.

1. BHADRASANA

It is always necessary to feel good about relaxation responses. *Bhadrasana* is practised sitting upright on the floor. The knees are bent and splayed on to their full extent so that they are lowered towards the floor, and the toes and feet touch one another in the mid line. The arms and hands lie relaxed, gently covering the toes. The difficulty to start with will be to lower the knees as far as possible. A certain amount of rocking from side to side will help get the knees nearer to the floor. (Do *not* try to push them down with your hands.)

Keep the pose for five minutes, increasing to 10 minutes with practice, while concentrating on maintaining pendulum breathing. The eyes remain open and a dismissive attitude of mind is sought. Sometimes a mantra helps at this stage. A point is reached where the stretched and tense tissues complain. As this happens concentrate on the relaxed parts of your body and stay with this feeling.

2. VIRASANA

This is simple. Kneel with hands (palms) resting on knees, the feet separated enough to allow the buttocks to reach the floor. Maintain this position for five minutes, increasing to 10 minutes with practice, while pendulum breathing is maintained as in the *Bhadra* position. Again tension and relaxation can be contrasted. Stay with the latter feeling.

Day Six

GROUP

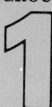

3. SARVANGASANA

a. Lie on your back with a folded blanket under the shoulders.

b. Slowly elevate the body until the trunk is vertical, the knees flexed so that they touch the forehead.

c. Finally, extend the legs out straight so that the trunk and legs are in a straight line. During these manoeuvres press the upper arms into the blanket and let the hands find their way behind the shoulder blades to support. The chest is pressed up to the chin as far as possible.

d. Hold the pose for a few minutes while practising pendulum breathing. With considerable practice this period can be extended to 10 minutes in a fit young person. There is little relaxation in this pose, but it will flood in as you move into your autogenics.

63

Day Six

GROUP 1

Autogenic component

This is a modified session of pendulum breathing. Repeat a simple mantra, 'My breathing is calm and regular', with each swing of the pendulum.

Some Group 1 people find that they prefer to rerun the whole autogenic programme on Day Six, focusing on the heavy limb routine (Day One), then the feel-warm routine (Day Four), followed by the regime described above. The completely inward-looking autogenic component contrasts well with the yoga poses and the two seem to work well together in bringing about the relaxation response.

1. NECK RELAXATION

Relaxation of the muscles of the neck poses certain problems. The head support muscles at the back of the neck and the head-twisting muscles must be identified and felt in tension and in relaxation.

a. Lie in your usual relaxation position and learn to recognize tension in these muscle groups with the tips of your fingers.

b. On Day One you identified muscle tension and related it to the *proprium*. Now you have to learn to recognize the state of tension only so that you can 'unlearn' it. This learning phase should not be over-long because it is the unlearning of this feeling that you have to master. There are so many proprioceptive messages involved in the balancing of a very heavy head on a relatively delicate neck bone structure that complete neck muscle relaxation is physiologically impossible except during deep anaesthesia. In neck relaxation you have to look for, and reinforce, such relaxed muscle groups as best you can. When relaxation of a muscle group poses a problem it often helps to go back to an earlier stage. Relaxing the arms and legs, so difficult to start with, helps to spread the process to other muscles. Eventually most of the neck responds to a simple working through of leg and arm relaxation processes, together with pendulum breathing.

2. FACE AND HEAD MUSCLE RELAXATION

a. This is more simply learned. The furrowed brow or anxious frown of the frustrated and anxious face is easy to feel and thus possible to relax in the normal 'feel it to lose it' routine. Sometimes if problems persist read the Group 3 section for Day Six and use these face and head massage routines (1 to 4). The muscles around the mouth and cheeks respond quite easily. The relaxed mouth is, remember, one that is ever so slightly parted.

b. Eye specialists doubt if there is such a condition as 'eye strain'. But many victims know the symptoms of strain around the eyes only too well, despite what the doctors say on the subject. The feeling of tension in eye strain is experienced if you look at a finger held about six inches (15 cm) in front of your nose and then gradually raise the finger until it disappears from your field of vision. The eyes are, of course, moved by muscles, and another set of muscles controls the eyelids and skin around the eyes. Relaxation of these muscles is experienced by looking slightly down (a demure glance) and by saying, 'My eyes are falling back a little into their sockets.' See also page 144.

GROUP 2

3. SHOULDER AND TRUNK RELAXATION

Neck and shoulder tension are often related, and shoulder tension is released quite easily by the following manoeuvre which is carried out in the sitting position.

a. Clasp one hand in the other behind the back at the level of the sacral bone between the buttocks and do the following two tension-producing movements.

b. First try to draw your shoulders together forwards as far as you can. They will indeed move forward a few inches. Hold this position for 30 seconds and then release the tension. Stay with this relaxed feeling for two minutes of pendulum breathing.

c. Then try to get your elbows as close together as you can behind your back, still keeping your hands clasped. Hold this for 30 seconds and then relax. Stay with this relaxed feeling while practising pendulum breathing.

GROUP

2

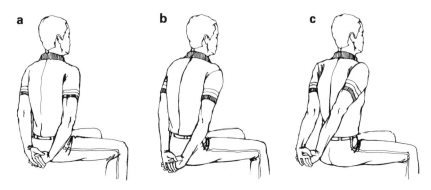

Although both these movements use the 'feel the tension first' principle which is not ideal for learning relaxation, such exercises are extraordinarily useful ways of mastering otherwise difficult shoulder and trunk relaxation.

Allow five to 10 minutes for neck and face relaxation learning, and complete your day's relaxation regime with a few minutes' pendulum breathing.

Take up a comfortable sitting position. Have a clock handy and time the following routine as accurately as possible.

1. HAIR SHAMPOO FRICTION

With fingertips of both hands give the scalp a vigorous shampoo-rub, concentrating on the hairline area, wherever that may be. As you breathe in (pendulum breathing) rub lightly, becoming firmer as you breathe out. Continue for about two minutes.

2. HEAD IN HANDS

Take up a head in hands position with the palms of your hands over your eyes. Pendulum breathe this way for two minutes, then gently give yourself a fingertip friction over the eyebrows with one or two fingers. The pressure should just be enough to move the skin. Continue for two minutes, then return to head in hands for a further two minutes of pendulum breathing.

3. NAPE OF NECK

Place the fingers of both hands on either side of the back of your neck, close to where the neck joins the head. Give deep pressure strokes slowly from the centre outwards as you pendulum breathe. Concentrate on any especially tense areas. Continue for two minutes.

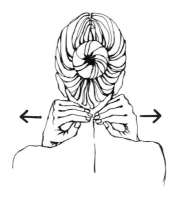

GROUP

3

4. EYE ROLLING

A curious but very useful strain-relieving exercise when combined with pendulum breathing. The whole exercise takes about two minutes.

a. Start by 'looking' around the edge of your field of vision in a clockwise direction. Make this a slow exploration, one complete circle for each in and out breath. After five such circles start your eyes travelling anti-clockwise for another five circles.

b. Then close your eyes and stroke across your closed eyes with your fingertips 10 times while pendulum breathing.

5. DIVE

a. Pretend you are about to dive into a swimming pool. Sit comfortably, push your arms in front of you as far as they will go.

b. Then push your arms back behind you as far as they will comfortably go. Maintain this position while you pendulum breathe five times (you will experience some curious proprioceptive shiverings in your arms as your body wonders what is expected of it.

GROUP

3

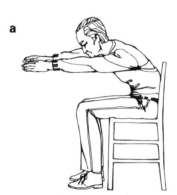

a

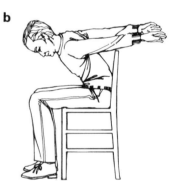

b

c. Now let your arms 'gravity fall' and dangle, allowing your chest to fall forward to your knees. Maintain this position for five pendulum breaths, savouring the relaxed feelings.

d. Repeat for two minutes.

Stand up to do the last two exercises.

c

68

6. STAND AND SHAKE

Stand comfortably, legs slightly apart, and shake out the tension from hands and lower arms. Continue for two minutes. Then keep the hands still and pendulum breathe for two minutes.

7. OPTIONAL EXTRA FOR THOSE WITH GOOD BALANCE

Carefully balance on left foot and shake out right foot and ankle for one minute. Then stand and pendulum breathe for one minute. Repeat with other foot.

8. PENDULUM BREATHING

Spend the rest of your half hour in your usual relaxation position, pendulum breathing and staying with your relaxation feelings.

Note

A quite unexpected degree of relaxation will be experienced during the rest periods after these exercises.

GROUP

3

ALL GROUPS

Mostly Revision

You are now deeply into your self-selected relaxation programme and well on the way to learning the basic relaxation techniques. At the heart of it all is, of course, the even pendulum type of breathing. If you are in any doubt over the technique reread Day Two, for without pendulum breathing the relaxation response is very difficult to experience.

By now you will have realized that we are using relaxation techniques as a trigger process that programmes your whole being towards the state of natural relaxation – the very opposite to the get up and go feeling. Both of these body states are entirely normal, natural and necessary. The pace of life in the latter part of the 20th century, however, has deemed it necessary for most of us to have to relearn how to relax.

At this stage of the 10-day plan you will probably be getting to know which of the very varied relaxation techniques suits you best, and for the rest of the time you will be refining your self-selected course to met your needs. Although you should always concentrate on the areas that you have experienced difficulty with during your training, because we are all so different you should also consider rejecting unhelpful exercises. If it seems that your group does not suit you in one area, then by all means stray into another one. Something there may build itself into your own pattern of relaxation.

Again I stress that it is important at this stage actively to select and refine, as well as to try to master the more difficult areas. Remember that for relaxation to be of lifelong use to you, *you* have got to take unto yourself a quick and efficient technique that you can turn to – and switch on, as it were – at the drop of a hat whenever stress and tension start to disturb you. At the moment you are still learning, so half an hour once or twice a day is necessary to establish a pattern. As you proceed you may find that one particular exercise or technique may 'turn you on' as far as the relaxation response is concerned. If it does, that's fine. Return to it. It is the key for you.

Selection from yoga-type programme

This is called a yoga-type programme because it merely takes a few of the classic yoga concepts and marries them to a relaxation technique. Classic yoga is in essence a Hindu philosophy and seeks a union with the supreme spirit. Yoga (from the word yoke) stresses this binding together, with the object of progression down a common path. It relies on abstract meditation and mental concentration. Many yoga techniques involve breath control, but in our mastery of the relaxation response we use breathing as the centrepiece around which we build a particular exercise, rather than as an ascetic practice. In other words, the 'yoke' of our yoga is a binding together of pendulum breathing with muscular procedures, aimed ultimately at the experience of the relaxation response.

In half an hour's relaxation the following yoga techniques can be managed in the first 20 minutes.

GROUP

1

1. STAND, STRETCH AND BREATHE

(Day One/Three)

2. LEG BALANCE AND BREATHE

(Day One/Three)

3. AEROPLANE (1)

(Day Two/Three)

4. SIT AND STRETCH, PRESS-UPS AND CHEST TWIST

(Day Four)

5. BHADRASANA OR VIRASANA

(Day Six). Devote 10 minutes to either *Bhadrasana* or *Virasana*, during which you may find a selected mantra useful.

Autogenic component

The autogenic side of the programme is an excellent complement to yoga. Autogenics literally means instructions made to yourself by yourself; it focuses attention on one part of the body while pendulum breathing is maintained. This allows the relaxation process to be initiated and for intrusive outside thoughts to be kept strictly where they must reside – outside the relaxation programme.

Be selective at this stage and concentrate for 10 minutes on *one* of the autogenic principles you have practised, either:

1. The heaviness of an arm (Day One).

2. The warmth of a limb (Day Four).

3. The regular calm character of breathing (Day Six).

The final components of the autogenic programme will be practised on Days Eight and Nine.

Start by reconsidering the relationship between the relaxed muscle and the relaxed self. Most of the therapeutic (medical) uses of the muscle relaxation technique have concentrated on the fact that both emotional disturbances and bodily symptoms of anxiety are accompanied by excess muscle tension. Even our language reflects this and we talk of so and so being tense or 'twitchy'. This book moves you a pace or so away from this concept and teaches prophylactic procedures to prevent symptoms being manifest.

Signs of excess muscle tension can be seen in the wrinkled forehead, the crossed brows, eyelids that twitch. When a doctor tests the reflexes of such a person, these are accentuated and extra brisk. A tense person can lie in bed apparently still and tranquil – especially if he is taking tranquillizers – and yet be as tense as a finely-tuned violin string. Not until unconsciousness supervenes – say, as a result of an anaesthetic or deep sleep – does he truly relax.

The method of pendulum breathing that you have learned, together with a planned programme of muscle relaxation, can produce complete relaxation without any dimming of your consciousness. In such a relaxed state emotional disturbances cannot bother you. Of course you will not want to spend any substantial part of your time in this relaxed state, but it is possible to learn to switch into relaxation at will to cope with tension in all its forms. It has been shown that the relaxation response is very powerful medicine. In the doses you are receiving it can only do good. Pressed to excesses – maybe to deep relaxation practised for several hours at a time each day – it has been known to produce hallucinations.

Your daily relaxation routine should now include:

1. Taking up your relaxation position, followed by five minutes of pendulum breathing with or without a mantra.
2. Feeling leg relaxation – noticing the strange proprioceptive feelings in the legs as they relax – but without carrying out your earlier Day One tension-making activities.
3. Relaxing hands, forearms and upper arms (Day Four).
4. Relaxing face, eyes and mouth muscles (Day Six).
5. If shoulders feel tense and difficult to relax, sit and carry out the shoulder and trunk relaxing exercises (Day Six).
6. Finally, allow yourself five minutes of a laid-back general relaxation, visiting parts of your body and enjoying how relaxed they feel.

As well as revision on Day Seven, we introduce hip and leg massage. The routine should fit comfortably into half an hour.

1. PENDULUM BREATHING

Start by pendulum breathing for two minutes.

2. HIP MASSAGE

a. Stand up, legs slightly apart, and place your hands in the small of your back. Without moving your head or shoulders rotate your hips in a 'hula-hula' movement. Plan one rotation for each pendulum breath.

b. After six hip swings in one direction, repeat for a further six in the other direction.

3. LEG MASSAGE

People vary greatly when it comes to how well or how badly they can reach for their feet and lower legs. For this exercise it is best to sit on the floor and flex one leg over the other. Wear shorts or pull up your skirt over the knees, having removed stockings or tights.

a. Place the right foot on the floor crossed over the left leg. Rub your right knee between your hands while concentrating on pendulum breathing.

b. Then vigorously rub your calf between the palms of your hands.

c. Then 'shake out' hands and fingers, five times each hand. Repeat with other leg.

a   b

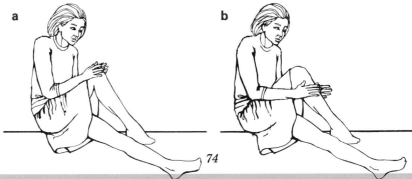

74

4. FOOT MASSAGE

Remain sitting on the floor in the *Leg massage* position.

a. If you can do so comfortably, massage between each toe, and finally pull the toe away from the foot gently before rotating the toe five times.

b. Then stretch out the foot straight and slap it down flat on to the floor five times, holding the knee to reinforce the action.

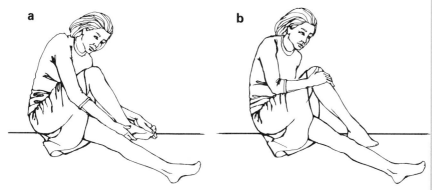

Repeat with other foot five times.

5. PENDULUM BREATHING

Have 10 pendulum breaths while sitting on the floor.

6. ARM RELAXATION

Sit in a chair, take 10 more pendulum breaths and then carry out the arm relaxation routine learned on Day Four.

7. PENDULUM BREATHING

Sit and carry out 10 more pendulum breaths.

8. HAND MASSAGE

Carry out the Day Three hand massage (Swedish regime).

9. PENDULUM BREATHING

Sit and relax with 10 minutes of pendulum breathing.

GROUP 3

Day Eight

GROUP 1

Yoga component

Today you should involve yourself with some of the more energetic yoga exercises, having first of all practised *Stand, stretch and breathe*.

1. STAND, STRETCH AND BREATHE

Stand, stretch and breathe for five minutes.

2. ROCKING

a. Sit on the floor, legs outstretched and together. Put your hands behind your knees, as if you were going to pick them up, levering the chest and head forwards as you do so. You are now in a position to rock backwards and forwards as you carry out pendulum type breathing.

b. As you rock back your feet should be rather higher than your head. Breathe in as you rock into the feet-high position, and out as you rock back to a head-high position.

a

b

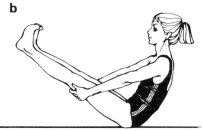

To start with it is difficult to keep the legs straight doing this exercise, but gradually a timed rocking can be developed that is graceful and preconditions the body for the next autogenic session. Maintain the rocking for five minutes.

76

3. BHADRASANA

Take up *Bhadrasana* pose (Day Six). Keep this for a further five minutes and then move to autogenics.

Autogenic component

1. Run through 'heavy' exercises, 'warm' exercises, calm breathing technique, and then move to 'cool' autogenic practice.

2. Concentrate on the forehead and repeat the phrase 'My forehead is cool', and then 'My face is cool'. As with the 'warmth' autogenics this phase takes some mastering and may not be experienced by everybody. Provided there is no panic to succeed, and any attempt at desperate striving is firmly rejected, the repeated auto-suggestion of experiencing forehead and face coolness is often successful. This is a particularly useful facility as it points you towards finishing your autogenics session feeling alert as well as refreshed.

To start with a full 20 minutes will be necessary. If you are pressed for time it might be best to economize on the yoga component.

**Day
Eight**

**GROUP
2**

Concentrating on feelings

By now you will have thoroughly learned how to feel the difference between a relaxed and a tense muscle, and you will realize that as muscles truly relax so does mental tension and stress. We started with exercises that focused on the legs because they give the easiest introduction to this experience. Today we will establish a systematic, easy to remember, relaxation programme for the whole body.

Because you know the feeling of a relaxed muscle, you can start with some 'difficult' muscle groups – head, neck and shoulders – and proceed to less difficult exercises in a simple top to toe manner.

Positions: Wherever possible in an exercise schedule it is a good idea to learn to relax on a couch or on a bed, or on the floor. You should also get used to relaxing on your back and on your side. This will give you added expertise in switching on to relaxation from tension at almost any time and in any circumstance. Start while lying flat on your back, and then repeat in another position.

1. HEAD AND NECK

a. Lie on your back, arms by your sides.

b. Press your head and elbows into the floor. As you lift your upper trunk slightly the back of your head and your elbows will feel its weight. Do this firmly but without straining. Lift on the *in* breath of your pendulum breathing.

a

b

c. As you exhale, drop back and savour the relaxed feeling.

78

d. Only do this exercise three times. On the fourth time *imagine* you are doing the tension-producing manoeuvre and again savour the relaxed response with a further three breaths. Then take six breaths, keeping with the relaxed response feeling all the time, but not remembering the exercise.

You will have spotted that you are again using the muscle-relaxing trick to learn the relaxation feeling. I have been careful, however, to reinforce the relaxation learning feeling in a way that overwhelms the tension side of the exercise.

2. HEAD ROLL

While you are still with the relaxed feeling, roll your head slowly from side to side practising pendulum breathing as you do so.

3. LIE RELAXED

a. Take up your original lying on back position. If you are tense you will find your elbows are close in by your side. (Instinctively you are trying to keep small and provide your enemy with a minimal target.) Now move your elbows away from your body, placing your hands just below your ribcage. Practise 10 pendulum breaths while appreciating how much more relaxed your arms, hands and fingers now feel. The more you ease your elbows comfortably away from the body the more relaxed you feel.

b. If, when you first take up this elbows-out hands-on-body position you find yourself clasping or feeling your body, then remove your hands from their clasping position and open and shut them five to 10 times quite quickly. Then let your hands fall back on to the abdomen. They will feel much more at rest and easy.

Having mastered these three points, repeat as many times as you can on your back and on your side. You may have some trouble doing exercise (1) on your side. In principle the feeling is the same but the muscles of the upper arm and shoulder, at first on one side and then on the other, provide the 'motive power'. When you try to adapt exercise (3) to lying on your side, gravity is allowed to let the free arm tumble forward across the chest to the floor or bed. The fingers are instinctively relaxed in this manoeuvre.

4. LOWER AND UPPER ARM RELAXATION

Repeat your arm muscle relaxation programme from Day Four.

GROUP

2

Day Eight

Your relaxation system was worked out by showing you how to relax muscles by means of various simple self-massage techniques. It is comparatively easy to self-massage a hand and arm, and the technique of massage and breath control will have been helpful. We then moved on to slightly more difficult areas.

As you have now learned that a planned system of self-massage can be relaxing and easy, it is time to devise a more systematic self-massage system. Here are a few possibilities – pick whichever ones come easy to you.

1. FACE AND NECK MASSAGE

1. *Hair shampoo friction*
With the fingertips of both hands give your scalp a vigorous but light shampoo-type rub (see Day Six). As you breathe in rub lightly, and as you breathe out rub more firmly. Pause after five pendulum breaths and compose yourself for *Head in hands*.

2. *Head in hands*
a. This is a little different from the exercise learned on Day Six. First, gently feel with your fingers around your eyebrows and eyes, your cheeks, your jaw and the underneath of your jaw and upper neck. Feel the residual tension.

b. Then switch to *Head in hands* (Day Six), when your nose just peeks out between your little fingers.

c. Then slowly move your hands firmly over your face until they now 'muff' your ears. Take a pendulum breath *in* as they do so.

d. Then as you pendulum breathe *out*, draw your hands down the side of your cheeks to meet under your jaw, and into a 'prayer' position.

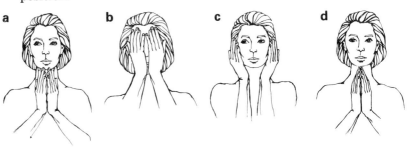

a   b   c   d

Repeat five times. Repeat the muscle tension feeling and gauging that started the exercise. Stay with the relaxed feeling you appreciate.

80

2. NAPE OF NECK MASSAGE

a. Place your middle three fingers of both hands in the nape of your neck and give deep pressure strokes outwards, moving your whole hand gradually, taking a one pendulum breath in and one pendulum breath out for each deep rub or stroke. Repeat five times.

b. Then let the head 'nod' forwards. It may creak a little but let it nod gently forward five times and then repeat the exercise together with the head nods. The second lot of nodding will be deeper than the first lot, due to more efficient muscle relaxation.

3. ARM RELAXATION

Next turn to Day Four and carry out your arm massage regime.

4. AUTOGENIC RELAXATION

Then lie down and give yourself 10 minutes' autogenic relaxation recommended for Group 1, Day One. Autogenics may well prove a useful end to your relaxation response sessions from now on. That is, if you have mastered this particular type of relaxation.

GROUP 3

Day Nine

GROUP 1

Yoga component

Gradually your group has fully developed a repertoire of yoga-type procedures. Day Nine gives you a chance to revisit certain components before you adopt your regular routine on Day Ten.

1. STAND, STRETCH AND BREATHE

Start by practising the slow *Stand, stretch and breathe* for five minutes, synchronized as usual with pendulum breathing. Many people in this group find that this exercise alone is enough to prepare them for relaxation.

2. LEG BALANCE AND AEROPLANE

Move into the *Leg balance* and *Aeroplane* manoeuvres if you have found these effective.

3. ROCKING

Then concentrate on the *Rocking* exercise first introduced on Day Eight. If this is going to be a feature of your relaxation in the future concentrate on straightening the legs.

4. BHADRASANA OR VIRASANA

Finalize your yoga-type exercises, and finish with at least five minutes in the *Baddha* or *Virasana* pose. In all probability you will have decided on your mantra, but if you need more guidance turn to Chapter 3.

Autogenic component

Some people find the self-teaching of autogenics impossible without a personal tutor; others take to it like a duck to water. Today you must perfect the best way to move around in your autogenic-based relaxation technique. Follow the programme you have got to know. Start with your heavy limb sensation, which by now will be easy. Having thus heavily relaxed, most of you can move through the warm exercise, repeating several times 'My arm is warm', as the mantra was repeated in the yoga pose. Although breath-control in pendulum breathing is used as a background to all relaxation, still leave yourself a good five minutes for your 'My breathing is regular',

'My breathing is calm', 'My breathing feels good' instructions to yourself.

At the end of the period proceed to the cool face, cool forehead exercise – blending this, as soon as the coolness is experienced, into a final autogenic instruction that says 'I am alert and refreshed'.

Indulging in a few good stretches, first of all in your favoured autogenic position and then a final stretch while standing 'feeling tall' as you did on your first day, is a good finale.

GROUP

1

Day
Nine

GROUP

2

1. BACK-RELAXATION (PELVIC TILT)

a. To start with, practise relaxation of the back muscles, lying on your back on the floor and trying to make as much contact with the floor as you can.

b. Press down into the area of the pelvis, below and to the right of your tummy button, and as you do so roll slightly to the right with your pelvis. This allows your left thigh to leave the floor slightly. This in turn tilts the pelvis slightly. It is a tension position so only stay there momentarily. Arms should remain relaxed throughout.

c. Then allow yourself to fall back into the total floor contact position. This feels nice and relaxed in comparison. Stay with this relaxed feeling for two pendulum breaths.

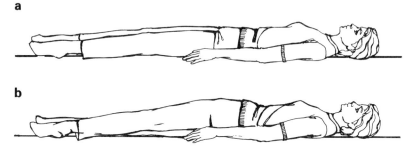

Repeat the exercise on a breathe-in and tilt, breathe-out and relax, routine two or three times. Then stay with the relaxed feeling for a few more breaths. This manoeuvre gives a useful bridge that takes you way back to the very beginning of the course when on Day One leg relaxation was practised.

2. LEG RELAXATION (PELVIC TILT)

a. By now you can feel a tense leg muscle and all you have to do is to switch it to *relax*!

   Having mastered the pelvic tilt, practise tilting the pelvis first in one direction and then in the other a little further, perhaps for three times. The tension you felt in learning the tilt will gradually be lost as the tilt persuades the thighs to relax easily without having to stress them, as you did in the original lift and drop leg exercises. Let your hands stay by your sides as you do this and stay with the memory of your relaxation.

b. As you do the pelvic tilt you must concentrate on synchronizing it with your pendulum breathing. While you learn this, let the feeling of the tilt first with one leg and the other get into some sort of rhythm, then concentrate on matching it to a four-second breath in and then out.

c. A natural progression from the pelvic tilt also relaxes the calf muscles and the difficult-to-relax muscles on the front of the legs. Before long both legs are well relaxed and then you can stop your exercises, staying with the relaxed legs feeling, so different from how they felt when you started the session.

3. FOOT RELAXATION

Finally, the feet need attention. Feet are used to remaining tense for long periods, and possibly this is why they are so difficult to relax. A good tip is to try a little 'grow longer' guile on them. Working on the principle that when we are relaxed we don't have to be screwed up and tiny, push heels as far away from you as you can. At the same time also push your toes out sideways firmly. Before long that 'I'm relaxed' feeling will start to creep into your feet too.

GROUP

2

Day Nine

On Day Eight you went through half of your consolidated self-massage routine. Now you complete the process by returning to your Day One routine, but in a slightly new form.

1. FACE AND NECK MASSAGE

Having built up a whole body regime on Day Eight, take it as far as the *Nape of neck* massage (exercise 2).

2. HAND MASSAGE (ORIENTAL)

Then, instead of going on to practise the Day Four routine, repeat Day Three Oriental regime.

3. HIP MASSAGE

Now move on to Day Seven and practise the *Hip massage* 'hula hula' movement.

4. AUTOGENIC RELAXATION

Finally, turn to Day One, Group 1, and practise the autogenic method exercises recommended there.

It is worthwhile making this tour of the sections today, for Day Ten is the last day of the course and time for you to make your final selection of what is best for you. You must choose for yourself the procedures that bring about the relaxation response in you, and also better and more comfortable living.

GROUP

3

Your Final Programme

You have now reached the end of your instructional course, and you should use Day Ten to decide exactly which of all the different procedures you have experienced suited you best. I do not want to dictate at this stage or make up your mind for you as to how you can most effectively plan your individual 30-minutes-a-day programme, but from what others have said, and from personal experience, I would suggest that the following could act as a template for you to work to. However, you are the only person who knows and feels instinctively which way you should go.

Having got your relaxation response well and truly tailor-made for *you*, do not be surprised to find it change gradually with practice. Suddenly you will be feeling, '*that* really works for me' or 'I don't think *this* routine is helping much'. Expect this to happen. It is evidence of your inner self talking to you perhaps for the first time in years. Learn to trust your feelings and instincts in this way. All that I have been trying to do for you is to unlock the doors of your own private relaxation therapy centre. Then you can stroll through the treatment rooms and settle in the one or two that make you feel good – really good and relaxed and at one with yourself.

Material that will act as a backdrop to the whole process of the relaxation response is dealt with later in this book. Already you may have been tempted to look ahead. And before you pick your final routine it might be worthwhile to read the rest of this book now, but if you do not want to get into the subject any more deeply then that is up to you and what you know now is quite workable and acceptable. Many hundreds of people have found the relaxation response they need by using only the information imparted so far.

Day Ten

Yoga component

When we started on Day One we had to begin somewhere, and as our self-selected group is composed of basically practical and energetic people we started with a yoga-type exercise and later moved on to synchronizing this with pendulum breathing. Now in your final programme one way of proceeding is as follows.

1. STAND, STRETCH AND BREATHE

Start off with *Stand, stretch and breathe*, concentrating as much on the breathing as on the exercise. *Leg balance and breathe* was really designed to underline the difference in feeling between tension/ strain and relaxation/comfort. It can usefully be omitted from a daily programme, but perhaps returned to from time to time.

2. AEROPLANE

Once the feeling of being tall is with you, many people in this group will find it helps to proceed to the *Aeroplane* exercises on Day Two. About five minutes should suffice.

3. SIT AND STRETCH

Then *Sit and stretch* (Day Four), dropping your head and trunk into the space between your knees in time with your pendulum breathing. After four or five, sit for a few breaths concentrating on the relaxation contrast of your experience.

4. PRESS-UPS AND CHEST TWIST

If you are young and energetic take up Day Four *Press-ups*, followed by *Chest twists*. If you are not so energetic move straight on to 5.

5. BHADRASANA OR VIRASANA

Repeat the yoga-type poses that you tried on Day Six. Many people find the *Bhadra* pose – sitting upright with knees bent and splayed outwards – the most effective of the poses described. (Incidentally, it is the most common pose in oriental statuary.) For those whose personal anatomy makes external rotation of the thighs at the hip joints difficult, *Virasana* – the kneeling pose – can be useful.

6. SARVANGASANA AND ROCKING

Many people will find that they can switch to *relax* quickly and easily by taking up a yoga pose without any preliminaries, and students can indeed leave the yoga component of their relaxation programme at just this point. Others, more energetic and more supple, may proceed to the *Sarvangasana* (leg high; Day Six) pose and the *Rocking* exercise detailed on Day Eight, before ending their 15-minute session in the yoga style.

Autogenic component

The autogenic credo of instructions made *to* yourself *by* yourself can form a very important contrast to the active yoga exercises. Doubtless the heavy/relaxation elements of the autogenic programme, together with the concept of relaxed and regular breathing techniques, are the most important part of the procedure. Often this 'autogenic package' can be grafted into the schemes for Groups 2 and 3 if these seem to stick at any point or become boring, tiring or tedious. Real autogenic enthusiasts have little difficulty in experiencing the 'hot' and 'cold' part of this type of exercise, and use the 'cold' experience as a useful and refreshing return to the world.

Always give yourself a chance to revisit pendulum breathing. Reread Day Two should the message have become a little dim. Short periods of pendulum breathing are always worthwhile.

Day Ten

GROUP 2

Now is the time to select what you believe to be the best starting place in your muscle relaxation programme. This will be your regular entry point into every relaxation session, and will move you rapidly into mastering total body relaxation. The main objective is to get rid of any sensations that arise in muscles, or in the joints that they control, and everybody seems to fall quite naturally into their own best method.

Try to develop a switch-off system that does not rely – as it did to start with on Day One – on feeling tension. (On Day One it was only experienced so that we could subsequently dismiss it.) Sometimes simply saying, mantra-like, 'let it go', or 'fall limp' or 'heavy' helps to silence certain muscle groups. A few breaths of pendulum breathing always ushers in the relaxation response, and you should start with five to 10 breaths. The following well-tried regime may suit you admirably.

1. UPPER LIMBS

Relax upper limbs, starting with hands, and followed by arms. The principle of 'opposite-handedness' is a good rule to follow, for the more dominant side of the body is the more difficult to relax. So if you are right handed learn to relax part of the left side quickly, and then transfer the feeling to the other side. You will find that relaxation breeds relaxation.

2. SHOULDER, HEAD AND NECK

Move on to shoulder and head and neck relaxation as described on Day Six.

3. LEG RELAXATION

Finally move to leg relaxation as detailed on Day One, but omitting the tension part of the exercise. Alternatively, use the Day Eight *Pelvic roll* if that worked well for you.

Moving into an everyday routine

Because Group 2 is comprised mostly of busy people with very full lives, the optimum and most advantageous relaxation situations may prove difficult to obtain. It is, therefore, a good idea to practise a muscle relaxation routine that suits the body when it is in a position dictated to you as you sit in a chair.

1. PARTIAL RELAXATION

a. In the sitting position, take up an accentuated floppiness – as one person I know puts it, 'like a drunk asleep in a train'. In this position the head flops on to the chest, the legs are slightly parted, with the thighs rotated outwards to a degree. The arms hang over the chair rests. (This latter position, although highly useful as a total 'let go' attitude, can in the unconscious sleeping person be traumatic and damaging; in some chairs the nerves of the arm can become compressed by the sides of the chair and a temporary arm paralysis can ensue.)

b. Once the relaxation response is experienced when sitting in a chair, your body position can be tidied up considerably. I always stress that chair relaxation can only be really effective if you make a thorough and repeated tour of your muscles as you sit there. You will be conscious of new proprioceptive impulses received from your muscles and your joints that are different from lying-down relaxation. Some muscle groups will, in fact, not be as relaxed as they would be in the 'drunk' or 'sleeping chair' position.

Such a concept of partial relaxation is very useful, and particularly so to those of us who spend a great deal of time in sedentary occupations. Personally, while my right hand is scurrying across the paper and my fingers contract as they grip the pen, I can feel perfectly relaxed in my left hand and arm, and well relaxed too in my legs. Exactly how relaxed you can get in 'second best' environments depends on many things, including the sort of person you are and your powers of detachment from the environment you are experiencing.

It is unlikely, however, that chair relaxation will prove to be totally adequate and rewarding without some regular sessions of *total* relaxation (which means spending some 15 or 20 minutes a day on relaxation training procedures associated with pendulum breathing).

2. KEEPING TO THE PROGRAMME

Once you have finalized your programme be prepared to stick with it for a few weeks, but do not be surprised to find it becoming less complicated as you master the relaxation response. The ultimate aim is to be able to enter into deep relaxation as easily as you can don a comfortable jacket or step into a pair of carpet slippers. This can only occur with training and regular practice.

GROUP

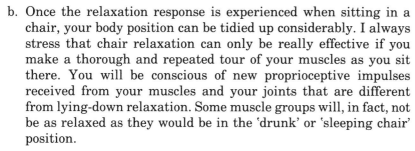

Day Ten

GROUP 3

In this important group we have proceeded along a training programme that was dictated by the following premises. First of all, muscular exercise and muscular activity are not predominantly a part of everyday life. This being so, the manifestations of tension are less likely to be muscle-orientated. Therefore, we concentrated on communicating with the proprioceptive system that tells us about our internal self by means of sensations generated in the skin. These, in turn, are reflected in changes in muscles, and thus, in turn, in the various internal body systems that control such important functions as blood pressure and heart rate.

Many of those people who self-selected themselves into Group 3 have some degree of disability. Some will, indeed, lead restricted lives as a result of their disabilities, but this does not mean they cannot be helped. The Group 3 programme has been designed in a way that most of the procedures described can be carried out by all members of the group. Naturally enough, this has dictated that you have to concentrate on areas of the body that are easily accessible to hands and fingers. For those of you who are fortunate enough to have helpful and caring partners or attendants, extensions of the programme are detailed in Chapter 9.

A good overall programme for Group 3 would include the following components:

1. HAND MASSAGE

Having mastered pendulum breathing, concentrate on your Day Three hand massage exercises and build these into your everyday routine as a 'starter', or to follow your optional warm-up.

2. ARM RELAXATION

Next turn to Day Four and add the arm relaxation component.

3. AUTOGENIC COMPONENT

Move now to the autogenic method that was introduced to Group 1 on Day One, and which is also helpful in your group. After 10 minutes of autogenics – which you can, with benefit, follow through to the complete 'waking up refreshed' programmes detailed for Group 1 on Days Seven and Eight – turn to:

4. HIP, LEG AND FOOT MASSAGE

If at all possible graft your Day Seven regime (exercises 2, 3 and 4) on to your routine.

5. HEAD AND NECK MASSAGE

Alternatively finish your programme with Day Eight *Hair shampoo*, *Head in hands* and *Nape of neck*, and finally read Day Ten chair relaxation in the Group 2 section on page 91.

Because Group 3 is composed of completely different characters, you will notice that we have unashamedly raided other groups from time to time to steal whatever might be useful from their routines.

Note

As I have already said, if you are having medical treatment for blood pressure, or a heart condition for instance, you must let your prescribing physician know that you have taken on a relaxation response type of training. There is no danger in the method but it might be necessary to reduce the quantity of medicines and drugs taken daily once the relaxation response has been mastered.

GROUP

CHAPTER 3

The Mantra

The part that the mantra plays in certain aspects of the relaxation response was only sketched in lightly in the 10-day plan. This follow-up chapter explains the mantra in more detail.

The word *mantra* is a relatively modern one. It first entered the English language from Indian writings during the 19th century. Literally, in Sanskrit, an 'instrument of thought', the word mantra has become synonymous with a passage from a sacred text, especially one from the Vedas that is imparted by a *guru*.

Veda, the name given to a body of knowledge which Hindus believe exists eternally, and which was made known to mankind by inspired prophets and seers, is recorded in a series of books known as Vedas. The most ancient of these were the Rigveda which dealt with praises or hymns, the Samaveda which concerned itself with chants and tunes, and the Yajurveda which dealt with sacrificial rites and formulae. From these 'roots of knowledge' more elaborate and systematized systems of religious practice developed.

From our point of view, in relation to the mastery of the relaxation response, we need not involve ourselves much in the intricacies of religious knowledge or dogma. It is perhaps an accident that the word mantra has crept into the subject at all. Many Eastern religions are linked with meditation techniques, and the modern occidental student of such techniques is often given a mantra by his oriental master as an aide, some would say a charm, to be used practically as well as spiritually in his task. Now the word has stuck and is used in ways that are often remote from its ancient meaning.

A mantra may have a powerfully mystical persuasion, and it may serve as a link between the truly religious and the purely secular. A really effective mantra will enjoy what is the essence of all mantras – a friendly, well-known and trusted form of words, the intrinsic meaning of which (if any) is not too important when the mantra is in use.

A formula of said or sung words is common to many sects and it is worth-while remembering that originally incantations were used as methods of healing as well as to bring rain or to rescue someone from peril. Only comparatively recently have incantations tended to acquire implications of sorcery. Previous to this they were quite respectable theologically.

Dr Herbert Benson, in his book *The Relaxation Response*, takes his readers by the hand and guides them through what the early Christians had to say on the mantra-like methods of removing themselves from the phenomenon of personal awareness. This awareness of oneself, as well as the intrusion of unwanted thoughts, is for some people a formidable obstacle to the learning of the relaxation response. St Augustine's principle of 'forceful turning away' from the thoughts that interfered with his own much-desired contemplations works well for some people but not for others. An anonymous 14th-century monk sought out and found 'special ways, tricks, private techniques and spiritual devices' which were also to be prized when other methods failed. One such spiritual device was to concentrate on the repeating of the single syllable of the word 'God' or 'Love'. This word, if 'clasped tightly into the heart ... shall be your spear [and with it] you shall strike down thoughts of every kind and drive them beneath the cloud of forgetting.'

As religious thought evolved in Europe, interest in the mantra principle increased. Martin Luther, for example, suggested the Lord's Prayer or the Ten Commandments as a suitable mantra. In fact, these comforting ancient words work extremely well if re-hearsed a little so that they fit gently into the basic background of the pendulum breathing rhythms. Simple prayers learned in child-hood fit into the same category: for instance, 'Gentle Jesus meek and mild. . .'

The 'Prayer of the Heart' was devised for simple lay people and dates back to ancient times. The priest of the Greek church who first used it in the 4th century might well have done so with 20th-century relaxation techniques in mind for he encouraged his flock to:

> 'Sit down alone and in silence. Lower your head, shut your eyes, breathe out gently, and imagine yourself looking into your own heart. As you breathe out say "Lord Jesus Christ, have mercy on me". Say it moving your lips gently, or simply say it in your mind. Try to put all other thoughts aside. Be calm, be patient and repeat the process very frequently.'

When the concept of a mantra was first discussed in my introduction to the 10-day plan I mentioned the poet Tennyson who experienced a profound change in his mode of everyday thinking simply by learning to relax while repeating his own name over and over again. Doubtless countless people have been trying to reach for ways to achieve the relaxation response since the beginning of time, and many have succeeded by the use of a mantra. For those who are interested in oriental philosophy and religion, a *given* mantra from a seer or guru may well be an added bonus. For others, short phrases with an intricate but not too intellectual charm seem to work best. Always the mantra must fit easily into pendulum breathing. The good mantra does not stimulate the mind or provoke thought. It comes to be welcomed as an old friend – some would say a charm.

SIX OCCIDENTAL MANTRAS

On either side of the river lie
Long fields of barley and of rye,
That clothe the wold and meet the sky;
And through the field the road runs by.

Tennyson

A slumber did my spirit steal;
I had no human fears:
She seemed a thing that could not feel
The touch of earthly years.

Wordsworth

Tyger! Tyger! burning bright
In the forest of the night,
What immortal hand or eye
Could frame thy fearful symmetry?

Blake

The Pride of the Peacock is the Glory of God;
The lust of the goat is the bounty of God;
The wrath of the lion is the wisdom of God;
The nakedness of woman is the work of God.

Blake

God be merciful unto us, and bless us;
And shew us the light of his countenance,
And be merciful to us.

Book of Common Prayer

The lord shall preserve thy going out,
And thy coming in,
From this time forth,
And even for evermore.

Psalms

Understanding The Stress In Your Life

CHAPTER 4

Good stress and bad stress

By now, or quite soon if you have not yet completed the 10-day relaxation plan, you will be able to relax at will. With some more practice you will be able to relax at any time too. However, the 10-day programme did not examine the reasons *why* you were so tensed up in the first place, and that is what we will look at in this part of the book.

Anxiety and tension are closely linked and, like every other fundamental human mechanism, they have been programmed into us by Nature for some good purpose. But sometimes, due to reasons that are not always obvious, people experience an overdose – or rather a distortion – of good, useful tension. And so the 'good' stress that we all need to make us get things done gets warped and twisted and we feel anxious, worried and tense.

Let us take anxiety first. *Anxiety* is primarily a state of mind closely linked with primitive survival behaviour. If we think that something unpleasant or hazardous is likely to happen we experience fear, and this naturally makes us feel insecure and 'bad'. Such an instinctive fear reaction is experienced by the body as anxiety – we want to fight or flee from the cause of the fear, and the symptoms experienced will be related to priming us for this reaction (see page 103).

One of the symptoms of anxiety that we commonly experience is a feeling of *tension*, in which our muscles are wound up to a high pitch of excitability. Tense muscles can of course cope with rapid action in the anxious situation in which we find ourselves.

Stress is a biochemical phenomenon that is to a large extent hormone controlled, in that the body uses chemical messengers originating in the nervous system to put into effect various voluntary and automatic body functions. The hormones are thus ideally priming the muscles and organs within the body to behave in an appropriate way to the degree of stress that is being experienced. However, inappropriate body reactions and mechanisms are experienced by all of us from time to time, and when these reactions become a major part of our experience of the outside world this is thoroughly bad stress, the type of stress that damages and destroys.

The trick is, of course, to use *good* stress to our advantage and yet prevent *bad* stress from spoiling our lives and making us ill. We know today how bad stress can act to our disadvantage. For example, excessive stress encourages the system to pour adrenalin and adrenalin-like substances into the bloodstream in excessive quantities. This upsets us in many ways. One of the effects is to disturb the internal body chemistry to such an extent that a porridge-like substance called cholesterol collects within the arteries to the heart and clogs the circulation. Then, when the heart is asked by Nature to increase its action, the restriction of its blood supply brings on the cramp-like pain of angina or even a heart attack because the heart is being denied the vital oxygen it needs to function.

Recent research has shown that there is a long incubation period between the first experiences of bad stress and the day when this stress-induced cardiac damage occurs. Various factors other than stress are also involved, for example smoking, diet and exercise patterns. This long incubation time can be both a disadvantage and an advantage to our health. It is long enough for the victim to put off doing anything about it; the stress symptoms are 'conveniently' ignored and he or she gradually but relentlessly goes downhill. But advantageously it gives time to intervene in the process as well. One important intervention is, of course, the relaxation response (see Chapter 13).

Are you specially prone to stress disease?

We all encounter stress but some of us cope with it more easily than others. A theory exists that there is what is called an A-type personality who is particularly prone to stress-producing disease. Such a person is:

1. A go-getter, loves competition, has a dominating personality, wants to succeed at all costs, is a quick and efficient worker.

2. Has a high aggression quota in his or her personality, gets cross easily, moves and eats quickly, is impatient, gets angry if delayed or kept waiting.

3. Is very time-conscious, wants to get things done quickly, likes deadlines (so they can be beaten), gets upset if idle and likes to fill up time with closely-tailored multiple schedules.

Those who believe in this theory believe that to escape the hazards of excessive stress such men and women should go about changing their ways in order to become B-type people who are the very opposite in personality make-up. I have found that to get these leopards to change their spots is usually impossible, and even if you do partially succeed, the A-type personality really despises his new persona. Better in such people is an understanding of the Human Function Curve, a concept put forward by a London cardiologist, Dr Peter Nixon.

THE HUMAN FUNCTION CURVE

The idea of human function curves shows how we all in our everyday life get things done as a result of a vital force that we call arousal (good stress).

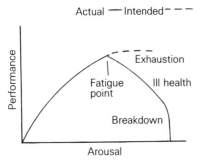

The Human Function Curve: Average

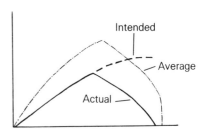

The Human Function Curve: High

The Human Function Curve: Low

As the diagrams show, three types of curve can be envisaged. They all have certain similar characteristics. With increased arousal (good stress), performance increases roughly in proportion to the degree of arousal until a point is reached where fatigue sets in. Immediately performance falls, and if more arousal occurs exhaustion sets in. This is followed by ill health (stress-related diseases), and finally breakdown.

Not all the human function curves are the same. A man or woman with a high curve can increase performance by increased arousal to a greater level than might otherwise be expected. High curves are enjoyed by those who have been carefully trained and disciplined on a long-term basis. Good mothering, security at work and at home, a well-rooted life in a stable society with a fair modicum of confidence, success and acclaim allow for high performance to be reached without ill health intervening.

But for those who get involved with bad stress on a long-term basis, performance, although heavily whipped by arousal, soon starts to fall off, and exhaustion, ill health and breakdown occur very rapidly. Low curves are predisposed by poor education, low social status, poverty, unemployment, less than good parenting, loneliness and lack of roots both physical and emotional. Low curves can be transiently produced by temporary and environmental factors – for instance extremes of weather, anxiety, overcrowding, lack of success in an endeavour, marriage breakdown, divorce, bereavement and grief. In other words, low curves result when things are going badly for you.

These human function curves are mobile things and not fixed like the A-personality leopard and his spots. In fact, we probably all function in our day-to-day lives within several variable curves.

The secret of using the function curve to advantage is first of all to heed the fatigue warning – the point when extra effort fails to bring about what we expect of it. By building a regular relaxation routine into everyday living we can encourage our body to function much more efficiently before the point of tiredness and subsequent exhaustion sets in.

The recognition of stress

Because we use (good) stress to help us lead effective and worth-while lives, the recognition and evasion of bad stress should become part of intelligent living. The following (bad) stress checklist may start you thinking. Bad stress may be signalled (in code) in the following ways.

1. *Upset mind symptoms* – increased irritability or restlessness – often associated with indecision, putting things off, getting behind with things; the 'can't get anything done' feeling; feeling tense, unable to cope or concentrate.

2. *Upset emotions symptoms* – becoming very fussy, suspicious, touchy, weepy, gloomy, a 'thorn in the side' of others; becoming a busybody; needing to be a member of a group, laughing at others.

3. *Loss symptoms* – loss of appetite, loss of interest in sex, loss of interest in job or house, loss of enthusiasm for usual pastimes, loss of sleep.

4. *'More' symptoms* – more drinking and smoking, more sex (including casual sex), or more tension feelings.

5. *Overaction body symptoms* – changes in your relationship with your body in which a normally quiet or well-behaved system suddenly makes itself 'felt': *excessive heart action* (palpitations); *bowel upsets* (overaction, especially indigestion, nausea, swelling problems, constipation sometimes); *muscle tension upsets* (experienced as backaches, neck aches headaches); twitching of muscles (eyes, legs); *tiredness of body*; *breathing problems* (sighing, can't get enough breath in, sometimes wheezing and asthma).

It will help if we take a deeper look at these common body symptoms because we can recognize how normal bodily reactions have been exaggerated and distorted to make us feel bad. Alongside the symptoms are the basic mechanisms by which anxiety is generated.

Common physical symptoms associated with anxiety that produce tension symptoms

SYMPTOMS	MECHANISM INVOLVED
Heart thumping, palpitation	Adrenalin and adrenalin-like substances are being released in relatively large amounts into your body. Your heart rate increases and you are conscious of its action. Your body is being primed for action – to fight or to flee.
Sweating and perspiration	A reflex action is making you slippery – hard to catch hold of. Basically a flight reaction.
Stomach cramps, loose bowels, vomiting, dry mouth, 'can't swallow', 'something stuck in the throat'	Your body has adjusted its gastro-intestinal tract for subsequent muscular activity. Digestion stops, the many sphincters (valves) in your digestive and eliminaton system go into spasm. Your body wants as much blood and vital nutriment as possible to be put at the disposal of the muscles. In extreme cases there may be involuntary emptying of the lower bowel and stomach (by vomiting): you may feel sick and be unable to face food.
Desire to pass water; that tensed-up, twitchy feeling	A similar mechanism to above. Other muscles are also put on alert at times. Sometimes you can see them complaining (eyelids and calf muscles twitch spontaneously). Writing deteriorates – is almost unreadable at times.
Inability to get to sleep	The body wants to keep alert for the emergency it expects.
Pupils look large	Pupils are dilated by adrenalin so that vision is as 'wide' as possible.
Jumpiness, over-reaction to sounds – telephone, door rattle, and so on	The whole hearing system is primed to catch the first sound of an attack on you.

FIGHTING, FLIGHT AND TENSION

On glancing through these common symptoms of anxiety a very justifiable reaction is to think, 'OK, I can see how in Nature stress, anxiety and tension helped in this primitive "fight and flight" response. But how does it apply to me? Nobody is after me with a hatchet or a spear. I am not about to pick a fight with anyone either – at least not physically.' A moment's reflection, however, must demonstrate that looking at the primordial feeling which is anxiety in such a simplistic way is unrealistic. All such basic gut reactions have two sides to them: they can be constructive (good stress), but they can also be destructive (bad stress).

Many people who are particularly prone to anxiety and tension profess to be fatalistic and subscribe to a 'What will be – will be' philosophy. This is fine as far as it goes. But if we consider that fate has something unpleasant in store for us we tend to be dominated by fear. This makes us feel instinctively 'bad' and insecure, and so we expend quite a lot of nervous energy trying to push such feelings into the background of our conscious mind, and our instinctive fear reaction is experienced by our body as painful and unpleasant anxiety – and of course we experience the tension that goes with it.

A decade or so ago, when the Biafran struggle was being reported in the newspapers, lorries and tanks were shown decorated with the motto 'No condition is permanent'. No doubt the Biafrans took comfort from this simple slogan, but it also reminded many people of the fact that life from its very inception is menaced by imponderables, and from the moment that we take in our first breath until we breathe our last we are to some extent in the hands of the chaos of Nature. It is a thought hardly likely to calm the anxious breast, but a certain peace of mind can follow a simple acceptance of this very obvious fact.

BUILDING UP CONFIDENCE IN YOURSELF

Learning to control tension and anxiety bit by bit, realizing all the time that you are making only small steps forward, is possible for everyone, however threatening the mechanics of life may seem. The relaxation procedures I have outlined will help, and whoever masters tension has understood the essence of all anxiety.

After the gentle *control* of tension has been appreciated, another step has to be taken. *Control* is also a yoke in itself. It binds the controller to what is controlled: the master and the servant, the hunter and his prey. Although control is a useful learning device, real freedom is harder to grasp and is bound up with the experience of true and lasting confidence in oneself. Confidence does not come solely by learning methods and, useful as they are, they are only buttresses to a true experience of reality and an awakening of a new kind of trust – *the essential trust in oneself.* Once you learn to trust yourself it is possible to accept the thrill of fear without magnifying it out of all proportion by adding tension and anxiety to it and thus making it unbearable.

The ultimate conquest of tension and anxiety implies an acceptance of reality and a sort of selfless loving of oneself. It is pointless to try to believe that the same way of experiencing this real freedom applies to all and sundry. Some find their inner peace through devotion and prayer, others through being able to laugh, especially at themselves. Whichever way you get there, a thoughtful conscious process is involved which is helped by a mastery of the relaxation response. This will eventually allow you to experience the dignity of the human soul that enables you to put fear, anxiety and tension in its place as you revel in your heritage of real freedom to live, love and explore your anticipation of a confident future.

CHAPTER 5

Anxiety
and how it
affects us

To understand anxiety we have to accept that it has components to it which are irrational. Its roots are often set in our childhood and upbringing. This is particularly obvious if we consider sexual anxiety. But it can be equally evident in more general fields. To want to escape from anxiety is natural, and the ways that we try (often subconsciously) to do so are also very natural. This case history demonstrates what can happen.

A young married woman was attending a psychosexual clinic. She loved her husband dearly, but an almost pathological shyness on her part was spoiling the couple's sexual relationship. Although they had been married for three years, her husband had never seen her naked and their lovemaking was always restricted to the dead of night and in the dark. As a result of psychosexual counselling, it came to light that, as a child, she and a young boy cousin had been caught 'playing doctors' by her mother. The game involved 'examining' one another with their clothes removed. The patient's castigation by her mother was both severe and prolonged and directed very much upon the 'dirtiness' and the 'forbidden' areas of the body that were so shameful that 'everybody keeps them hidden'. Although this childhood sex trauma had occurred 20 years previously, it was still powerful enough to remain a potent trigger for sexual anxiety in her adult life.

Sometimes we become aggressive, and fight some sort of battle to ease painful tensions. To feel more secure we can also transfer the responsibilities that make us feel so anxious on to other things, such as institutions or movements, or on to other people, such as doctors, children, social workers and priests. Often we do certain odd or strange things without realizing that the impulse that drives us to them is anxiety. At times we perform useful, honourable, worthy and brave acts without realizing that we are driven to do them unconsciously to master fear.

Perhaps the most popular concept today is the idea of freedom. The very terms 'freedom fighters', 'sexual freedom', 'freedom from want' dominate the headlines in our newspapers, as well as what we hear and see on radio and television. But to be truly free we have to be, to a large extent, fearless. Some men and women can indeed effectively control natural anxiety by fearlessness. For most of us such bravery is impossible; for us salvation lies closer to steering ourselves gently to a state of affairs where we can face fear and anxiety due to a closer understanding of how it effects us – the symptoms of anxiety in other words. Having identified the symptoms we can proceed with the treatment through relaxation. Then, hopefully, the anxious face with its lines of tension, its dilated pupils and suspicious eyes, can relax and even break into a gentle smile. It has been said that 'every smile is an expression of victory over fear and a reappearance of that harmony in which confidence balances anxiety', and brings with it a sense of freedom. Perhaps I should put this another way and say that every gentle smile is evidence of a relaxed person.

How to recognize anxiety

We know that anxiety and tension are normal states, so often providing the spur to, if not fame, then achievement or the giving of a satisfactory account of ourselves. But it is necessary to look closer at the darker side of tension and stress too, and to learn more about the destructive, damaging manifestations of anxiety. Only by doing this can we recognize anxiety and relate it to tension. If we are able to examine anxiety in our everyday life – catch sight of it unawares, as it were – and be aware of the mechanisms which make us feel ill and upset, we can often defuse it. A new kind of serenity, making mental pain and anguish appear like an old enemy we have grown to understand, can then be developed.

This knowledge of how we are affected by anxiety is, of course, not enough by itself. We have to use the knowledge to breed confidence, and to learn the relaxation techniques that fight the physical side of anxiety to win through and reduce its damaging effects. Our subconscious mind so hates deep-seated anxiety and tension that it often goes to quite elaborate means to hide them from our attention. To do so, however, 'costs us' in mental energy, and is a constant drain on our life force. All costs have to be met eventually, and to try to minimize these costs we often distort our lifestyle and develop various quirks of behaviour.

And so quite often plain anxiety and the tension it creates become transformed within ourselves and appear in strange guises. One such guise is associated with an unusual reaction to, or preoccupation with, either real or supposed deprivations.

TIME DEPRIVATIONS

An everyday example of a deprivation-produced type of experience is the feeling of (supposed) *time deprivation*. People caught up with this always seem to be in a hurry. They have to beat the clock, and however much time they have to do a job it is never enough. Such people have, in reality, as much time as anyone else to do what is necessary. But they feel basically insecure about what is expected of them and cannot feel freedom or voice this painful anxiety. Their subconscious mind produces a semi-comforting excuse for them: they are being deprived of time; it is not fair. And this is why, they point out, they are performing so badly. Of course, with all the rush they become tense and the very feeling of tension adds to their anxiety.

COMMON DEPRIVATIONS AND ANXIETY

Another way in which anxiety and tension is generated is the phenomenon of *contact deprivation*. The ease with which the inquisitor, the police questioner, or the torturer demoralizes his subject by means of contact deprivation is too well-known to be dwelt on at length here. Solitary confinement, bare comfortless surroundings isolated from anything that gives an indication of the hour of day, is the rule in such circumstances. Food is delivered through a slot in the wall. All these sensory deprivations of solitary confinement are potent generators of anxiety and tension. Happily, relatively few people are subjected to such conditions, but many find themselves in less dramatic circumstances undergoing the experience of loneliness and social isolation that trigger anxiety.

'Rehousing' the elderly and the infirm into social conditions in which they know nothing of their environment other than the confines of their own house commonly produces this type of anxiety. The loneliness of the unemployed person at home is another example, as is the loneliness of the emigrant worker, and the loneliness of the young mother with small children around her, but without close relatives or friends. The young housewife who has left employment for a few years at home raising her children often suffers both real and supposed deprivations that tend to generate anxiety. Although the disciplines of timekeeping and office or factory life are gladly abandoned, to start with at any rate, deprivation of social contact due to the loneliness of home life often triggers off anxiety quite unexpectedly; a neighbourhood that was previously only experienced at weekends, when it was crowded, seems strangely deserted from Monday to Friday.

The retired man or woman often suffers quite profound deprivation anxiety generated in a similar way. Even the bustle of getting to work is sadly missed, together with contact with office staff, customers and superiors. On top of the real social deprivation that occurs in the retired is the anxiety shadow cast by the thought and feeling of being supposedly deprived of one's *persona* – the feeling that one no longer *is* somebody of even small import. This loss of kudos (supposedly) in the eyes of the world often makes for a feeling of anxiety and depression. 'So much has been lost – so much have I been deprived of by retirement, illness or fate! Whatever will they deprive me of next? My very existence?' seems to be a commonly experienced feeling at such times.

All these circumstances are sensed subconsciously as a deprivation of human contact. That this is really a false or *supposed* sense of deprivation is no solace to the tense and anxious people experiencing this feeling. The world is there around them, as it is for everyone, but they feel they cannot take advantage of it. They feel deprived, and unable to mix, join in and take part in life. Their 'deprivation' is generally a private misery and yet somehow they almost enjoy feeling deprived in this way, for it 'explains' the agony of their tensions for them.

EMOTIONAL DEPRIVATION

Sometimes feelings of *emotional deprivation* produce quirks of behaviour that are seemingly inexplicable. The squirrel complex of the hoarder who cannot throw anything away may be symptomatic of this sort of basic anxiety. Only by hoarding can he escape fears of being left with nothing. The compulsive millionaire moneymaker who has no capacity to enjoy his wealth is often someone who supposes himself deprived (of love). Being thought a worthy citizen or someone of true worth is the only way he sees to escape the tension and pain of his real situation. Convincing himself by the size of his bank balance that he is the sort of person he would like to be compensates for his other deprivations.

It is not going too far to equate the behaviour of the compulsive eater, or drinker, to feelings of supposed deprivation. The person who is tense, anxious and who feels deprived of love, and therefore 'worth', will draw comfort from greedy eating and excessive drinking. Only in this way can a sense of inner emptiness be assuaged.

This sense of inner emptiness is experienced to a considerable extent as tension. Somebody who experiences such feelings is saying, 'They have deprived me of my worth, the love and consideration that is due to me... They can't deprive me of this.' And so they have another drink or a couple of chocolate bars. If instead of allowing themselves to misread the basic cause of their problems in this way, the physical side of their symptoms can be managed by learning to relax – life assumes a rosier hue and self-confidence grows.

THE SUPPOSED INEXPLICABLES

For many tense and anxious men and women Damocles is alive and well. (Damocles, it will be remembered, was a courtier who excessively praised the worth of his tyrant ruler, who reciprocated by inviting him to dine with a sword suspended over his head by a hair.) The tense people who experience this Damocles syndrome are beset by the threat of disaster, rather than by anything actually hazardous or dangerous. A vague threat seems to hover over them like the sword of Damocles.

The anxiety and tension that is due to a vague and inexplicable threat has been well appreciated by story tellers and writers. In classical mythology, the hero Perseus 'knew' that if he actually looked at the awful Gorgon he would be turned to stone. To defuse its inexplicable dread he devised an elaborate trick and by using Athena's shield he was able to operate upon the Gorgon's reflection. The ancient writers of this tale tell us something not only about the primeval existence of the supposedly inexplicable fears, but also about the possibility of evading their power by turning aside. Perseus turned aside by using a reflection. If we can recognize the state of tension in our body that reflects an inexplicable fear, we can turn aside from it by relaxation.

For some of us, the supposed inexplicables that generate anxiety lurk in curious places – for instance, in a fear of uninhabited houses. There is often a link between phobias and the supposed inexplicables, for there is nothing real about the threats that phobias impose on us. The private hell of agoraphobia or claustrophobia, fear of heights, small animals, and so on are all evidence of what is sometimes called *free floating anxiety* (a fear of the unknown). This is dealt with by linking it to some (usually avoidable) situation or object. It is as if the mind were saying, 'I can't stand feeling so tense and anxious about *everything* any more – it's too painful! Instead I'll just be afraid of *something*, say spiders, and avoid them. Then anxiety generally will not upset me so much, as long as I avoid spiders.'

In many ways this psychological package deal is very effective. It is quite easy to avoid spiders – or mice or snakes. If, however, the phobia relates to the whole outside world, as it does in cases of agoraphobia, this is a different situation and the symptoms of tension (the symptoms of phobic fear) need to be dealt with in a different way. One way is by a system of desensitization, which is an acclimatization to the symptoms by means of the relaxation response.

Broadly speaking what happens is this. If for instance the phobia pertains to spiders, the victim is first shown pictures of spiders, films of spiders and so on while he practises the relaxation response. Then spiders in glass jars and models of spiders are handled, then tiny and larger spiders are touched and handled. The terrifying symptoms of the phobia are thus experienced first in miniature, and confidence is gained as the relaxation response helps to manage these symptoms. Later on the victim used his new 'coping' skills to manage his anxiety and tension in realistic situations.

It is most likely that we all use, albeit unconsciously, similar devices to cope with the fear of the supposed inexplicables – the fear of the unknown, the free floating anxiety of everyday life. The method selected by many of us is often a planned, if unconscious, exposure to the 'horrors'. The horror movie, the bizarre and chilling tale, the weirdness of science fiction are the modern-day equivalents of the old-style melodrama and the spine chilling tales of folklore used by our forefathers for rehearsing their coping skills.

A scientific example of the anxiety- and tension-producing possibilities of supposed inexplicables was reported a few years ago from a psychiatric research establishment in Chicago.

A group of patients, aged between 18 and 49, who were attending a psychiatric outpatients clinic at the Institute of Psychosomatic and Psychiatric Research and Training Hospital of Chicago, were asked if they would like to spend a full day at the hospital. No seriously ill patients were involved in the study, nor was anyone included who had recently been suffering from a psychosomatic illness.

During the morning hours of the experiment, psychological testing was performed, and the volunteers were brought into the laboratory and familiarized with what was to be for them a test situation. They lay on beds and electrical machines for recording blood pressure, heart rate and so on were attached to various parts of their anatomy by a 'friendly and reassuring' technician. When all was in readiness the 'chief' of the laboratory entered and ceremoniously checked all the equipment. Then after reassuring the patients that all was well he switched on a dummy complex of electronic devices that was clearly visible at the foot of each bed. Finally he told the subjects to be still and relax. The experiment had begun.

After about 15 minutes, noises of a certain and constant character were transmitted through the head phones that the patients wore, and the physical reactions were monitored. Then an unexpected anxiety-provoking procedure began. A mild electric shock was administered to everyone and various electrical noises were transmitted by a hidden loudspeaker. The chief rushed in and indicated that something of an inexplicable nature had happened. When complaints were made about the electric shocks, he told the patients to be very still as there 'was a lot of high voltage' about. Almost immediately small electrical spark discharges, accompanied by the smell of burning rubber, issued from the dummy apparatus. The chief then 'reassured the subjects in a manner indicating that he was far from sure of the validity of the reassurances'.

Eventually the experiment was concluded by the chief leaving the laboratory to 'cut off the current at a master switch'.

Leaving aside the questionable ethics involved in carrying out such tests on patients (judged as 'extremely successful in creating a frightening situation, in which subjects sighed, moaned, groaned and offered desperate advice about corrective measures and pleaded in quavering voices'), there seems no doubt that the quality and quantity of the anxiety generated came from the inexplicable nature of what was happening to them. The unknown factor in the situation predominated. Nobody knew what was to follow – more electric shocks, perhaps fire, personal injury or even death by electrocution.

The inexplicable fear of the unknown (how can we *really* fear something we have never experienced?) is of course felt in a wide variety of ways. The elderly person who receives an unexpected letter (what will it contain?) is at one end of the spectrum. The fear of death lies at the other. Acquiring knowledge of the trigger factors and the symptoms of anxiety, and learning how they can be assuaged by the relaxation response, is what this book is all about.

CHAPTER 6

Anxiety, tension and the lack of creativity

We have seen in the previous chapter how two factors – inexplicable fears and feelings of deprivation – stem from an internal mismanagement or poor handling of almost universal stress situations. But there are other important anxiety and tension trigger factors that need our attention if we are going to be able to recognize them at work in our lives, and so take evasive and therapeutic action against them (by using the relaxation response to defuse them).

The word tension basically means 'stretched', and anxiety means 'to throttle'. The 'overstretched' and anxious person will often say he feels 'throttled' or 'obstructed' by society, or by the boss, his spouse, government restrictions, regulations, and so on. A brief look at this basic foundation of anxiety and tension will give other useful clues as to methods of escape from anxiety in everyday life.

· Sometimes these throttled feelings produce aggression as a precursor of anxiety. So primal is this type of anxiety provocation that it is not difficult to set up simple animal experiments that show it in action. It is quite easy, for instance, to teach animals that by pressing a lever, or operating a door, they can gain access to food, and it is not too much of a stretch of the imagination to consider this to be a very simple creative act. But if, once the animal is thoroughly habituated to his nice little piece of creativity, instead of getting his expected food he occasionally receives an electric shock, the chances are that after the initial surprise he will react by aggression and will fight the door or lever. If the experiment is continued, a state of uncertainty sets in and the animal demonstrates psychological upset, twitchiness, tension, stress and anxiety brought about by throttled creativity and hunger.

The need to create something as part of everyday existence is apparently essential to our mental well-being. Some years ago the manufacturers of Volvo cars were looking for ways of combating boredom and inefficiency on their production lines, for a bored assembly worker is a difficult and anxious man to handle and is prone to aggressive reactions. Often such aggression is reflected in strikes and industrial unrest. Volvo found a way around this dilemma by arranging matters so that groups built their 'own' Volvos. In other words, they escaped the demoralizing repetitiveness of the production line and could instead see the end product they had created.

Many people are lucky enough to have jobs and occupations that have an element of creativity about them. This may be sufficient to keep anxiety and tension at bay. But if they are suddenly removed from such work – through job loss, retirement, or a reorganization which transfers them from their creative work to something more humdrum – anxiety and tension often manifest themselves quite quickly. (There would seem to be a strong argument these days for teaching the relaxation response to everyone in industry whose job is threatened, with a view to possible prophylaxis in the future!)

One of the less well-known examples of tension and anxiety being generated within a personality is what I call, for want of a better phrase, 'easy street neurosis'. What happens is as follows. A successful man or woman who has led a busy life, and has perhaps created a flourishing business, finds that a take-over offer is irresistible. Sensing what the personal loss of his brain child will mean, he often retains a position of some substance within the new set up. But rarely does this new position involve the same skills, responsibility and flair that created the original business. The (fortunate) abdication of a former arduous role convinces the 'victim' that in compensation, he will now have all the time in the world for golf, bridge, holidays, leisure – all the things that, for a busy person, were previously at a premium. Reality, however, is often disappointing. New and usually younger people are involved in the creative side of the new organization. The new position that the creator of the business has negotiated for himself is for the first time seen for the shell that it is. Such an abrupt loss of anxiety-assuaging creativity produces a sudden onset of tension and ill health. That is, unless suitable new creative activities and an understanding of how anxiety can be combated by relaxation restore the *status quo*.

Women sometimes experience a short sharp dose of 'easy street neurosis' when they least expect it – when finally, and often with a sigh of relief, their youngest child leaves the nest. Suddenly everything should be marvellous but in fact anxiety and tension move in and take over.

Retirement, too, if entered into suddenly and without proper planning, produces loss of work symptoms that are heavily laced with tension and anxiety.

Unfortunately, in our culture few people are lucky enough to live by their creativity. There is a tendency, too, to denegrate creative hobbies as being undesirably arty-crafty – often by those who really need them. Surprisingly perhaps, just those people who most often need some activity or hobby in tune with creativity, instead tend to spend their time and money in competitive tension-producing games and activities – for example golf, football, sailing and jogging.

Jogging is at the moment enjoying a popularity that is quite unrelated to its health-giving properties. The stressed and haggard face of the jogger who strives to push his body to greater and greater feats of endurance, pitting his stamina against the clock and distance, gives the lie to this being a really healthy activity. It is also a lonely sport devoid of any creative bonus.

Anxiety-assuaging creative activity does not necessarily mean the work of the painter, the sculptor or the potter, although such activities are indeed highly potent anxiety-reducing occupations. Somehow whenever the brain and eye are directly linked with the hand, in creativity, stress is spontaneously reduced. The quietly skilled dressmaker, the enthusiastic knitter, even the dedicated pastrycook, equally well demonstrate the power that an admirable end product has in assuaging anxiety. A similar feeling of being able to sit back and admire something one has created also helps the psyche of the do-it-yourself fanatic or the keen gardener.

Of course not every tense person is suffering from a sense of throttled and restricted creativity. Nevertheless, if you look at the artist, the successful performer, the confident and creative teacher, the proud gardener with his splendid lawn and basket of vegetables, you will very often see the contented and relaxed person. This happens so frequently that it is well worth remembering the positive and helpful elements of the creative process in the battle against tension and stress.

It is not necessary to be a creative person in the conventional sense to harness the power of creativity to fight anxiety and tension. The control of anxiety begins with thought and proceeds to action. Any personal 'project', an evening class, a new hobby, a drama class, has a built-in creativity bonus. Some find a warming sense of creativity by involving themselves in good works and charity jobs. If these are carried out without thought of personal advantage they can be truly creative.

Another often forgotten creative activity is the organisation of, and the participation in, the traditional family festival. To many the membership of a 'larger family' – a religious sect or body of the church – helps to fight anxiety both by the observation of ritual and by Faith. To 'take a Faith' increases confidence in the meaningfulness of life. Uncertainty is, of course, inherent in life, but through religion it is often possible to put one's trust in another Being. Such a positive trust allows many fears to be accepted and overcome – even the universal fear of death and dying. Perhaps a simple acceptance of reality, and the confidence that in a way there is a divinity within ourselves, is the greatest act of creativity that we can accomplish in the universal search we all make as we try in many different ways to seek the tranquillity of the truly quiet and selfless soul.

CHAPTER 7

The fear of reality

Tension creeps into our lives in many ways. Almost always in anxiety is the *symptom* we feel that turns us into tense individuals, often in a very baffling way. In the previous two chapters I have shown how several threads of fear, or modified and altered fear, permeate the substance of anxiety. First of all two subconscious phenomena were examined; one of which acted because of a sense of deprivation; the other which was preoccupied with the apparently inexplicable nature of things. In the last chapter the disruption of peace of mind due to a throttling of creativity was discussed. Now we must examine something which completes the picture of anxiety – a basic fear of reality, perhaps the worst culprit of all.

This may appear to be a paradox, for fear by definition may be expected to be either dissolved by cowardice or routed by courage. But this particular problem is a unique psychological one. It is not generated as the result of events; it is a fear of the mechanics of life itself. Thus it may be considered as a special form of anxiety and tension born of the real world which is patently not a source of worry to everyone.

Are those who experience this fear of reality different – perhaps only in some very slight way, or at rather special times – from the majority of people for whom everyday existence is accepted, if not always happily, then at least philosophically? In truth the nature of this difference, this foreboding about life itself, is very complex in some cases and very simple in others.

The simplest factor is due to what psychologists refer to as a straightforward lack of personality maturation. In the same way as a puppy will stop and bark at a piece of paper blowing across a street, various real-life and utterly banal situations can make the 'immature' person disturbed and anxious. The differences between the average non-tense individual and his tension-prone fellows may stem from various conflicts which he has not been able to resolve satisfactorily. Sometimes they have their origins in childhood, or even babyhood (see page 105).

I do not think it is necessary to attempt to explore the inner reaches of the personality too deeply or theoretically in order to repair some of the tension caused by this type of basic fear of reality. However, it is worthwhile to examine in a little detail some of the situations that we see around us, where in their everyday lives the 'victims' are trying to escape from this sort of tension.

Attempts at escape from a worrying reality

ALCOHOL

Alcohol might well be looked upon as a specific drug, tailor-made to ameliorate distressing symptoms of this particular form of tension – i.e. a basic fear of reality. It will not help very much, except in anaesthetic quantities, with the other types of anxiety we have been discussing, but as far as reality fears are concerned, it is, superficially at least, effective and efficient.

Alcohol is a selective and progressive depressant of the central nervous function. When taken in smallish doses it removes, temporarily but surely, the highest and most critical biological functions of the brain. Larger quantities of alcohol gradually inhibit the whole of the central nervous system until eventually a state of anaesthetic intoxication is reached.

The anxious and nervous 'social drinker' endeavours to limit his consumption to the first phase. Alcohol effectively dampens all the psychic phenomena which are responsible for his anxious reality fears, and he is transported, for a while anyway, into the easy world of his more fortunate fellow creatures. Sometimes this drug-induced confidence is of considerable value. One of the ways in which we learn to mature is by getting over various achievement hurdles, so if confidence does follow an excursion into the fearful world of reality as a result of a few drinks, then real confidence may subsequently develop.

Unfortunately alcohol does not seem to do this very often. Indeed, it is hard to make a convincing case for a 'cure' of this sort being brought about by any tranquillizing drug. This is because once the tranquillizing effect wears off an upsurge of anxiety always erupts. Sometimes this is referred to as the rebound phenomenon.

No one has satisfactorily explained the dynamics of alcoholism, but some people do progress from social tension-releasing drinking to straightforward alcoholism, in which life without the drug becomes intolerable and work impossible. The potential alcoholic is someone who drinks to lessen intolerable tension; the occasional drinker uses alcohol to increase the pleasure of living and maybe to get over a few maturation hurdles.

There is a useful comparison between the frequency of suicide and the proportion of alcoholics in the Western World, and there seems little doubt that the two are closely related. Some psychiatrists believe that alcoholism is an expression of a half-way house between an innate death wish (to escape from unbearable tension) and a natural tendency to overcome the tension. It seems likely that when fears of the real world are very incapacitating, the individual will clutch at any solution that seems to promise salvation (e.g. alcohol).

But the fears of real situations and the tensions that arise from them which alcohol can allay are usually overcome spontaneously if the individual is given time to cope with his environment. We often expect a young adult, not so very long out of adolescence, to behave with maturity very soon after finishing his formal education. Making one's mark in the world is for most people a fairly traumatic experience, and if the young adult is not over-pressed or harried into mature life patterns he will gradually find he does not need recourse to alcoholic or other indulgences.

Alcohol is available to everyone as a universal tranquilliser, and will continue to be used by those seeking a release from stress. Its consumption in Britain has doubled in the last 20 years, and the same pattern is seen in other developed countries. But unfortunately alcohol, despite its obvious attractions, is a poor investment return for the 8 per cent of all consumer expenditure involved in its purchase. No pharmaceutical company anywhere in the world would be allowed to market a drug like alcohol, which apart from causing physical disease if used to excess also impairs memory, causes brain damage, induces or releases aggression, leads to the breakdown of family life and often actually precipitates anxiety in its takers, even when only quite moderate doses are taken.

TRANQUILLIZERS

It is fashionable to regard the vast array of tranquillizers so commonly prescribed today as *specific* drugs for reducing anxiety and tension. Such a drug if it were to work efficiently would have to 'home in' on to a certain area in the brain that might be termed the anxiety centre. Unfortunately no such area in the central nervous system has ever been shown to exist, and so we must regretfully reach the conclusion that there is little if any difference between tranquillizers and other sedative drugs such as alcohol.

The perils of addiction to tranquillizers do not seem to be quite so devastating as they are to alcohol and other narcotics. All tranquillizers are to some extent habit-forming and dependence is common. Breaking the state of tranquillizer-dependence is always associated with an abrupt and often traumatic experience of the stress and anxiety that originally occasioned their usage. A far better and more natural way to cope with tension and anxiety is to re-educate the body to respond less unfavourably to its effects by means of taking advantage of the relaxation response.

SMOKING

Another self-prescribed stress intervention drug is nicotine, and here we are dealing with one of the most powerful and most puzzling drugs known to man. It is puzzling because it has a curious dual action. To understand the seductive nature of nicotine as an addictive drug you have to understand a little about the relationship between the automatic (autonomic) side of the nervous system and the conscious self, for whether or not we feel up or down, tense or relaxed, depends on this relationship. We have seen in the 10-day programme that there is a direct link between this 'feeling' part of the brain and the relaxation response. We have also learned that it is possible to influence the functioning of the autonomic nervous system (that controls heart rate, blood pressure, and so on) by means of directing the central nervous system (our brain) to feel relaxed and at peace (mainly by muscle relaxation and breath control).

Nicotine is unlike almost any other drug in that it has the facility of a dual action, taking place mostly at the various 'junction boxes' (synapses) that occur up and down the autonomic nervous system. In certain concentrations in the blood it helps in the transmission of impulses across these junction boxes, and so for instance increases the heart rate; at other concentrations it depresses the transmission and the heart rate falls. But together with this action there is another rather more interesting effect of nicotine – it is a powerful stimulator of brain activity. In excessive doses it can even produce the ultimate in stimulation of general brain activity and excitement in the taker – it can produce convulsions.

An example of this action in miniature is the sickness often experienced by the novice smoker, due to the stimulation of the part of brain concerned in vomiting. More sophisticated smokers will be aware of another stimulant effect of nicotine on the brain: heavy cigarette smoking tends to delay the production of urine and thus delays the rate of filling of the bladder. It does this by causing excessive production of a urine-diminishing hormone by stimulating the relevant part of the brain.

To understand the chemical lure of smoking it is also necessary to explore the way in which we self-administer nicotine. When doctors want a very prompt and dramatic action of a drug they pump it directly into the bloodstream; drug addicts involved with narcotics do the same as they *mainline* their heroin. Another extra-quick way to dose the body with a drug is to *mainline* it into the veins of the lung – where the drug in vapour form is only a cell's membrane away from the circulation. (This method of fast drug delivery is effectively used by doctors in the administration of many substances by aerosol.) The smoker thus *mainlines* his highly potent nicotine into his bloodstream, repeatedly puff by puff, maintaining a suitable concentration of the drug exactly where he needs it – in the 'feeling' part of his brain – thus producing the necessary 'high' he has conditioned himself to expect. This good feeling he comes to equate with other good feelings that he finds combat stress and anxiety.

Unfortunately, due partly to the dual see-saw action of nicotine on the whole of the nervous system, the good feelings associated with nicotine are very transitory. In other words, they alternate quite rapidly between good and relaxed, and bad and twitchy. They can, however, become constantly adjusted with an extra cigarette or two. Elsewhere in the body the things are not so easily 'managed' by the smoker. The one-tenth to one-fifth of a milligram of nicotine that the body absorbs into every litre of blood going through the lungs during the smoking of a cigarette brings about an increase in the heart rate of about 10 beats per minute. (The blood pressure rises too.) A secondary process liberates excessive quantities of noradrenaline into the blood. This noradrenaline may be looked upon as the fundamental stress hormone – the chemical messenger that instinctively prepares us for fight or flight, making us super alert, twitchy and jumpy.

Clearly therefore, although nicotine is a seductive and effective booster at a central level (in the feeling part of the brain), it presents the very opposite effect in other parts of our organism. Of course we do not 'feel' these stress effects as such. Smoking, therefore, fails as an anti-stress aid in the long-term process of healthy living, although it allows many people to cope more effectively and enjoyably with their day-to-day existence, their job and even their relationships.

GAMBLING

An association between two of the most prevalent addictions in Western society – between alcoholism and gambling – has only recently been appreciated, and the establishment of a gambler's refuge organization, Gamblers Anonymous, follows closely on the better-known Alcoholics Anonymous in its *credo*. The reasons that an individual turns towards gambling, which also may lead to social degradation, crime, and even suicide (when the inveterate gambler suddenly has to face the fact that he has lost everything) are extremely difficult for non-gamblers to understand.

The drinker, especially in the early stages of his habit, obviously gets some pleasure from his drink. The enjoyment may stem from a memory of the pleasurable world of friends and cronies in which the otherwise anxious hours are whiled away, or the times when good fellowship and sociability outweigh the tension and worries of the world. But the whole background of the addictive gambler is almost always unattractive and sordid. Bookmakers' premises are seldom, if ever, happy meeting places. Occasionally the amenities offered by high-class gambling establishments are pleasant enough, but the gambler rarely makes these part of his interest. If you watch the people who cluster round the tables in both elegant and ordinary gaming houses the most striking thing about them is a common air of detachment bordering on despondency. Watching a group of players as they lose large sums perhaps at the turn of a card or the spin of a wheel, it is difficult to believe that they are having an enjoyable experience. How, therefore, can we explain the fascination of gambling?

One explanation is that gambling provides a method of escape from anxiety and tension, an escape organized with some sophistication which removes the individual temporarily from painful concern about real-life problems. Although the actual escape mechanism is not fully understood, the gambler perhaps makes a package deal with himself which says: 'Reality and all it implies is too productive of anxiety and tension. It makes me feel bad to think that I am solely responsible for everything that happens to me. Gambling is different – it's luck, and surely I will be lucky today. Fate owes me this.' The essence of gambling is, of course, a continued flirtation with Lady Luck. *She* therefore becomes responsible for the gambler's plight, his failures and successes. Nobody can really pass judgement on a man or woman who is out of *luck*, whether at cards, dice, horses, or even the football pools. And so a measure of peace in the world is 'bought' by excusing oneself from personal responsibility for one's plight and all it stands for.

Unfortunately, gambling is rarely successful. Although sometimes an individual has a run of luck that beats, temporarily at least, the laws of chance, the odds are always weighed against the gambler. The stakeholder must earn a profit, or close. Many severe addicts will sometimes persevere quite relentlessly throughout a winning phase until 'bad luck' inevitably overtakes them again. Then they feel they have a justifiable excuse to escape from real situations, and withdraw to a world of the hard-done-by and rejected.

DRUG DEPENDENCE

The most frightening aspect of anxious flight from the real world and its tensions is the flight into drug dependence. In many ways there is a similarity between alcoholic flight from reality and drug addiction. However, in the case of the drug addict, personality deterioration is acute rather than chronic and hopes of remedial therapy rather less likely. The drug addict also places himself, by the illegality of his action, in a position which from the very start is a point or two further removed from the real world of ordinary people and happenings.

At the present time we talk about drug addiction under two main headings: addiction to soft drugs and addiction to hard drugs. As far as soft drugs are concerned there is pressure to place marihuana and cocaine, the most popular of these, in an intermediate position between the socially accepted addictions, like alcohol and tobacco, and the so-called hard drugs, by which we mean mainly heroin. Pressures have been brought to bear either to legalize marihuana smoking or at the very least to reduce and limit penalties for being in possession of this drug.

A quite convincing case can be made that long-term addiction to marihuana may well be less damaging to the health than heavy use of alcohol or tobacco. Although the long-term effects of marihuana are not well documented from the point of view of pharmacology and pathology, the most common short-term effect of the drug is a sense of dreamy well-being. Habitual use leads to a decline of personal ambition, a loss of sexual desire, a turning away from previously valued social ties such as family life, and a loss of pride in personal appearance. In other words, the addict once again makes a psychic package deal with his personality, and accepts willingly the effect the drug has upon him in return for his escape from personal anxiety about the real world.

PSYCHOSOMATIC ILLNESS

By far the most common way to escape a life which is itself a frightening and anxiety- and tension-ridden experience is by means of a simple mechanism which has nothing to do with any of the common social or other addictions. It is by a flight into self-imposed illness that restricts one's activities to those which are 'safe' if generally very boring. Every medical student, from his early clinical training, learns to differentiate between the symptoms of physical illness and those which are graced with the term 'psychosomatic'.

Physical symptoms can stem from a demonstrable pathology, a change in structure of an organ or tissue. Palpitation or rapid beating of the heart may follow the mechanical failure of this organ as a pump or may be due to diseases which have altered the structure of the heart valves or muscle. But probably the commonest form of palpitation is due to anxiety and tension. The symptom is a psychosomatic one in such cases.

Psychosomatic symptoms are often unpleasant. Apart from palpitation they commonly include fainting, shortness of breath, diarrhoea, paralysis or even blindness. Sometimes they are so devastating that it is difficult for lay people to understand what is gained by those who suffer them. Exactly what is gained, however, is often a relief from tension and severe anxiety.

At times the psychosomatic escape from a worrying reality fear is incredibly snugly tailored to meet the situation. The actress may be prevented from doing something with a heavy anxiety tag attached to it by loss of her voice. A student may be so anxious about the result of his examination that biliousness or diarrhoea prevent him from attending the examination hall. A mother who finds child-rearing difficult and full of anxiety may become very unsteady on her feet and complain of giddiness to such a disabling degree that she cannot be expected to cope safely with the little one.

An understanding of the nature of psychosomatic illness and its relationship to anxiety and tension is useful if it leads to an understanding of those stricken with these miseries. Clearly nothing can be gained by branding such people as 'inadequate' or even 'malingerers', 'lead-swingers' or 'scrimshankers'. One way they are likely to overcome their disabilities is by the gradual emergence of real confidence in themselves as people, and to learn comfort by relaxation rather than withdrawal.

Psychosomatic symptoms must be accepted for what they are: painful ways of deflecting an even more painful state – a state of extreme and painful tension.

THE POWER OF THE GROUP

Let us look at another pathological solution to the devastating symptoms of anxiety, which again involves a modification of life-style. One of the most alarming ways in which the individual can behave when faced with painful anxiety brought about by the stress of reality is by the destruction of the real situation. This is replaced with a less anxiety-filled reality. The process has a well-documented history. Certain countries prior to the last war, haunted by the social conditions of the age, set up totalitarian regimes which destroyed their social systems and even attempted to destroy races in order to create a new and reassuring reality.

A more prevalent withdrawal from reality today is a withdrawal into a special sort of conformity, a withdrawal into the group. It seems very likely that this instinct is responsible for the popularity enjoyed by many strange types of clubs and off-beat minority groups. Sometimes this is a harmless defence against anxiety and tension. But fashions change. The present club uniform is rather odd and many of us find it difficult to understand. The hair tends to be worn very long, brightly coloured and sculpted, or skin-short; the clothes are highly coloured, bizarre, untidy or excessively uniform. To the parent generation the aims of the club are inexplicable, and the means of achieving them questionable.

Nevertheless, it seems a shame not to make some effort to understand these social processes, for they evolve in order to try to ease reality tensions in a reasonably acceptable fashion. The football field or the tennis court have always been places where battles against a tension-filled reality are successfully waged.

CHAPTER 8

If you have tried to relax but relaxation does not seem to come as it should, it is worth asking yourself a few pertinent questions. There are several possibilities to consider. One is related to what psychologists call self image problems. In such cases you basically don't like yourself, and this dislike tends to preoccupy you – to the extent of not letting yourself accept the idea that you can do anything about how you feel. You feel tense, irritable and dispirited, and try as you will you can't relax.

Trouble shooting:
Have you a self image problem?

To understand such problems it is necessary to go back to when you were young. We all begin to store up experiences with the world in a fairly stereotyped way. To start with we have no way of telling the difference between ourselves and the world outside. But gradually we learn that parts of our body are ours and that if *they* are hurt *we* are hurt. As life goes on this self-awareness grows and eventually becomes organized into a highly sophisticated concept of self. At this stage we come to see the changing world from the standpoint of our constant self.

To see better how this happens, again let us consider childhood. First of all we learn a view of our self from our parents, and later from friends at school. People we work with help build this self concept too. If the view that others take of us is a favourable one we tend to develop a good self image. But the opposite also occurs, and when this happens we do not feel at all good about it. So much does it hurt that there is a tendency for all of us to make package deals with reality in order to preserve our body image in as favourable a light as possible. Sometimes to obtain this we do things that surprise us or even shock us. Sometimes we tend to behave in weird and wonderful ways to *compensate* for the damage that we feel has occurred to our body image.

Examples of this unaccountable behaviour are the very fabric of life and living. A man who has a bad self-image as a sexually successful person may engage in frenzied sexual and pseudo-sexual exploits to try to repair his self image. A similar state of affairs occurs in women too. A child who does poorly at school will often try to compensate for this on the games field. Sometimes, of course, such devices are highly satisfactory.

123

Some people, however, do not seem to compensate their way out of their self image problems. When this happens they try to solve the pain they feel in other ways. For example, if one's self image is disturbed because of what one considers to be unworthy motives (or sins), one way to alleviate anxiety is to rail against similar motives observed in others. This can salvage such an individual's self image problem to a large extent (proclaiming perhaps 'I may be bad but look at him!'), but it usually leaves the protester in a high state of agitation and upset.

Yet another emotional package deal is often set up by the person whose self image is being damaged by, say, an intolerant employer, spouse or colleague. He paradoxically reacts by identifying himself with his mentor, and so also becomes hostile and tense. He seems to be saying, 'I am the boss too in my own way. Look how fierce and nasty *I* can be.'

Another device common in this personal protection game is to displace our agony on to others. Such a person feels impotent to fight the real saboteur of his own self esteem and so he takes it out on others. A child may cruelly hurt the cat when he can't hurt mummy. A husband may hurl a damaging insult at his wife to make him feel a little better about how he sees himself.

WAYS OUT OF SELF IMAGE DILEMMAS

To try to ease out of this sort of problem is not easy, and the relaxation response by itsef is probably not going to be very helpful. So upset is the person who is trying to cope with a self image problem that the paraphernalia of relaxation is rejected before it has a chance to work. Quite a lot can be done, however, by starting to talk to yourself in a supportive way, if this is indeed your problem. To some extent you have to turn away from that old image. But if you feel, as many do in this situation, that you can't change after all these years, you just set yourself up for certain failure.

The past must be rejected in these circumstances, and life restarted with the present and future in mind. All too often we only take account of the things we do which go wrong: the relationship that has soured, the business project that has become fouled up, the dress that we didn't buy quite enough material for, the cake that somehow missed out on the sugar. Instead, we must remember to appreciate ourselves more for the good things we do. They may not be many or very impressive, but they *are* there. It's not just a case of self-righteousness to remember them.

An example springs to mind relative to a common subject of fractured self image – the failed dieter, or for that matter the slipped drinker. It's all too easy to dwell on the fact that you have failed in your endeavour, say after only 10 days. But this is negative thinking. Wherever you are *now* you did *succeed* for 10 days. Having done so, say to yourself that you can go on dieting or not drinking for another day, and having regained your self image a day or two or maybe a week can be added to your score. The difference between self-righteous behaviour (which is often so irritating to others) and the sensible repairing of a damaged self image is that in the former we want others to tell us how good we are, and in the latter we give *ourselves* the quiet credit – and credit always has a tendency to grow, very slowly at first and then by compound interest.

One way to change bad old self image problems is to plan for success. Set yourself a few goals in which you are bound to succeed. Some people who, say, want to build more exercise into their lifestyle aim to be two- or three-hour joggers. When they fail in the first half a mile their self image wilts. Instead, if they were to set a five-minute goal, or even a two-minute one, their 'notching' up of success would bolster their self image. This principle can be extended to things like slimming, painting the house (start with a shelf), setting the garden straight (prune a rose bush), or even writing a letter (a two-liner maybe)! The important thing is to select a goal and then achieve it with pride. Next time the goal can be more ambitious.

Those whose self image is severely dented – fractured even – need to work quite hard at their repair job, and start, as I've said, with small areas of remodelling. It's a good idea to get into a habit of self-review at this stage. Indulge in a sort of action replay of the things that worked for you today, maybe at bed time. Remember, too, how your self image evolved when you were tiny. It got good by small successes remembered (learning to read a new word or two). It got bad by equally small remembered failures (failing your two times table). Make sure that each day the remembered successes outshine the failures, even if you have to set yourself a whole range of instant successes to start with.

Some psychologists set great store by what they call guided imagery as a self image building process. Really it is a sort of daydream about the sort of person you are trying to be. It is said to work well for competitive sportsmen and performers generally. Most image-building success of this kind is due to rehearsal. Good 'spontaneous' speakers, whether they be at a prestigious banquet or at the local football club, do in fact carefully rehearse and work on their performance. If ever you hear even a famous actor do an 'off the cuff' speech the chances are that it will be awful. Similarly, preparation for an important meeting or perhaps a housewarming party pays hands down. Part of that preparation is, of course, in the mind. But practical measures are also relevant and important too. They contribute greatly to how you fare 'on the day', and how your self image feels about it afterwards.

Finally this image-building process must include taking full responsibility for where you are *now* without blaming yourself for it. Blame is self-defeating in this way. It gets you stuck deeper in the rut. You have to learn to view your failure – the things that have really hurt you – as opportunities to learn something new about yourself and about others. Once you really get down to this you are open for real improvement.

Before leaving this superficial 'look at yourself in a new light' exercise, always remember that there are others who can help when personal self image damage seems impossible to face alone. Don't be put off if these people call themselves doctors, psychiatrists, psychologists or counsellors. They are all members of the same species as you, and prone to the same pressures of living that you are faced with, although possibly in other ways. They have, however, developed special skills in problem solving. Skills are only learned to be used – and helping you feel better about yourself is their life.

Trouble shooting:
Are you depressed, or are you suffering from a depression?

It is always possible that somebody who is depressed might feel agitated and worried to the extent that they turn (or are turned by some concerned person) towards sampling the relaxation response as a way out of their troubles. Unfortunately the relaxation response will be a total failure in real depression, and it is worth while looking at the subject of depression in a little detail so as not to fall into this trap.

Psychiatrists talk about two types of depression. First there is *reactive depression*, well named for it is a reaction of the mind to something that has happened – usually something sad and upsetting like the death of someone near and dear, the end of a love affair, even a severe and catastrophic financial loss. Rather different is *endogenous depression* – a depression that typically comes on without apparent cause, although some such endogenous depressions seem to follow a virus illness such as glandular fever or viral pneumonia. Sometimes endogenous depressions are secondary to sudden hormone changes – maybe after childbirth or at the menopause. But for the most part endogenous depression comes from out of the blue and the victim has no idea what causes it, though it is probably some upset of internal brain chemistry.

It is important to contrast both of these types of real depressive illness with something quite different – just feeling depressed. We all get depressed at times. Life is characterized by its ups and downs, and it is very difficult to see the silver lining all the time. Sooner or later in the normal way of things our mood changes. Sometimes, however, the depressed feeling does not lift. The sadness deepens and the victim cannot snap out of it and becomes really (medically) depressed.

CHARACTERISTICS OF TRUE DEPRESSION

Classically in true depression there is an overriding melancholy associated with physical behaviour changes such as lack of energy, lack of appetite for food, sex and everything else. Even the stomach and bowels get depressed and indigestion and constipation are common. The head often aches. In severe endogenous depression there is loss of judgement, feelings of persecution, feelings of guilt and worthlessness. Sometimes hallucinations occur, or at the least a firm engagement with reality is lost. The deepness of the depression varies – it is worse in the mornings. Sleep is disturbed in a highly characteristic way for the victim wakes early in the morning, or even in the middle of the night.

If you say that such a person is unlikely to want to learn to relax or to be gently coaxed along such a path by friends and relatives, I would be the first to agree with you. But on occasion depression – particularly the endogenous kind – can start with a period of anxiety and tension. Dr Arthur Watts, who has probably done more to educate doctors (psychiatrists included) in the true understanding of depressive illness, stresses that anxiety is a much more common and misleading camouflage for depression than is usually recognized. He feels that about half of the cases of incipient depression present a picture of chronic anxiety and agitation in the eary stages. Here is where the relaxation response may be sought out and found wanting.

The centres in our brain that control the emotions and which are disturbed by depression are very close to those that control the automatic (autonomic) nervous system. This being so there is a considerable overlap in the symptoms of autonomic disturbance, like rapid heart beat (palpitation), uncontrollable shaking of the fingers (tremor) and excessive sweating, all symptoms that may well indicate that the relaxation response may be helpful. Unfortunately relaxation will not be helpful if it is a true depression that is expressing itself in this way.

Depressive illness can be present in so many forms that constant vigilence is prudent. A change in someone's behaviour may be the earliest sign of an incipient depression. A woman may suddenly embark on a series of unwise love affairs; a man may become obsessed with a gambling spree, or may behave in an uncharacteristically dishonest manner. If, together with this rather unusual lead in to a depression, tension is present too, then ways of relaxation may be sought or advised. But, as emphasised previously, they will be doomed to failure in such circumstances.

Sometimes a depression can be spotted by a friend quicker than by a doctor. An early sign is someone becoming no longer interested in their appearance. Hair is left to its own devices, shoes are never cleaned, stockings are worn into holes and not changed, dandruff remains on the collar, make-up is haphazardly applied.

MANIC DEPRESSION

One other variation of depression needs our attention. It is so-called *manic depression*, sometimes referred to as mania. In a way this might be looked upon as a pathological variation of the euphoria that all of us feel on our good days, when everything goes well, the sun shines and we can't think why everybody else is not singing in tune with us. When this euphoria gets out of hand, however, a worrying medical picture emerges. A person so afflicted, like the true depressive, begins to wake up and rise earlier and earlier. Often he starts energetically to get on with his routine tasks. In theory he should really be getting on top of things in a big way. Characteristically this does not occur. Such a person is so easily distracted that everything is only a quarter or half done. At this stage the mood is erratic, boastful claims are made, inappropriate singing or shouting may occur, spending sprees may be embarked upon. In some people sexual promiscuity becomes very obvious for a while.

In the early stages 'victims' will be able to see glimpses of how unusual their behaviour is. If not, friends and spouses certainly will draw their attention to the problem. At this juncture the relaxation response again may be thought of as a suitable remedy, but unfortunately again it will be ineffective and the sadness of true depression will eventually occur.

WHY THE WORRY?

One person in 25 will experience at least one episode of one of the depressive illnesses we have been looking at, which will be severe enough for them to seek medical attention at least once in a lifetime. Certain types of depression seem to run in families (endogenous depression). Always in such cases suicide is the gravest risk. Depression, in one form or another, directly causes two-thirds of the 4,000 cases of suicide in Britain each year. Late adolescence, middle age and post retirement age are common times for a depression to erupt – menopausal women seem to be particularly at risk.

There is an element of urgency, therefore, in getting depressed people involved in proper medical treatment as soon as possible, for modern drugs and electrical treatment are extremely useful. Waiting or trying ineffective treatments – like the relaxation response in this context – are too dangerous in the face of such dangers.

Trouble shooting:
Glandular problems and general illnesses

If something has gone wrong with one of your major body systems you are not going to be able to put it right only by learning to relax. This does not mean the same as saying that the relaxation response will not help you to cope with illness – generally speaking, the reverse is true as we see in Chapter 13. Most people have vague ideas that they are at the mercy of their 'glands' and that glandular problems are mysterious causes of ill health and mental breakdown. This is in no way true. However, there is one glandular illness that does give symptoms of anxiety and which may *seem* suitable for relaxation therapy. This is the condition of *thyrotoxicosis*, and it does not respond to the relaxation response.

THYROTOXICOSIS

The eary symptoms of this illness are agitation and a feeling that the whole system is going into top gear and yet you can't do anything about it. Quite soon, however, excessive fidgetiness, anxiety and tension supervene and most people suspect they are ill. With this comes disturbed sleep and a feeling of not being able to relax at all. The hands become shaky and writing deteriorates. All of a sudden everybody else seems to want to have the room too hot. The victim often opens windows and wears the flimsiest clothes. Even so he or she perspires and remains hot and bothered all the time. Often palpitation will be obvious and the heart races and flutters. Unexplained breathlessness is common. Often the bowels overact too. Appetite is good at this stage, but quite soon a feeling of weakness supervenes and a loss of weight becomes obvious. Eventually the body becomes so weary that even lifting up the arms becomes a feat of endurance. By now, in women (the disease is more common in females), the periods have stopped. Some people develop prominent eyes which appear staring and protruding.

Obviously in the early stages the victim may self-diagnose excessive tension and decide to treat the subsequent anxiety by means of the relaxation response. To start with a minimal improvement occurs, but eventually a medical diagnosis clinches the matter and proper remedial measures bring about a cure.

More Ways To Relax

CHAPTER 9

Relax with a friend

Although this book is mainly about teaching *yourself* to relax, for some people company positively encourages the relaxation response. For such friendly souls the following modified system of relaxation learning will help.

There is an ancient and well-founded tradition for hand contact being associated with a healing process. Many of Christ's miracles were associated with touch, and He doubtless knew of the art of healing carried out in the ancient world of Egypt and Babylon. The kings of England from Edward the Confessor onwards traditionally healed by touch, and this royal occupation was maintained until the days of Queen Anne, who, it is recorded, therapeutically 'touched' the great Samuel Johnson.

The beneficence of the touch of one to another is obvious throughout life. In the days when I saw a lot of children in my practice I found that if it was possible to make hand contact with the body of an upset baby or frightened child the battle was half won. Once as a young casualty officer I managed to introduce over 60 stitches in the face of a toddler who had been badly injured by a dog with no stronger 'anaesthetic' than a comforting touch first of all administered by me and after by a sympathetic young nurse. (She told me later that she was so surprised at the progress we made that she had suspected hypnosis.) Possibly the fastest way to soothe a frightened or restless child is to sit him comfortably on your knee and stroke him gently, like a cat.

Some of the wizardry of osteopaths may well stem from the fact that they have developed a healing touch, and certain doctors who practise the 'laying on of hands' as a healing process are clearly drawing on a power that is in many of us, should we care to develop it.

There is, of course, a world of difference from the touch of the masseur and the touch of the healer, secular or religious. But they do have one important thing in common: a close and appreciated contact between the hand of one person and the body of another. In this brief schedule of relaxation for two we make full use of this primitive and yet very modern application of touch.

It is important to realize that the degree of success that you obtain from your relaxation course will depend to a large extent on what you both put into it. Relaxing with a friend has an added bonus in that you both have a chance to be 'giver' and 'taker'. It is probably best for the partner who considers himself or herself to be more tense to start as the giver.

132

Massage component

Most modern massage is based on the techniques of the 19th-century Swede, Peter Henrik.

Physiotherapists and masseurs use several techniques that are not particularly beneficial in the context of the relaxation response, and so percussion 'hacking and tapping' form no part of this plan. We concentrate instead on stroking, both deep and superficial, together with gentle kneading and skin rolling. Occasionally frictions are helpful in certain areas too.

Massage is no good if the person receiving the massage has clothes on. The most skimpy underwear only can be worn if really effective massage is to occur, and the state of nudity is almost always preferable. Massage should ideally be carried out on a firm couch (not a bed) or on the floor, with perhaps a blanket over the carpet. The room must be comfortably warm. If the hair is long it should be tied back. Jewellery and watches should be removed, and the fingernails of both masseurs kept filed close to the tips of the fingers. Lubricants or talc may be employed, but are not necessary.

Some massage experts believe that tension-releasing exercises should be practised *before* massage. In this book I take the attitude that the massage sets the stage for a later exploration of the relaxation response.

After one partner has 'given' the massage and helped with the relaxation exercises the roles are reversed.

THE MASSAGE TECHNIQUES

Stroking

This can be *deep* or *superficial*.

a. *Deep stroking* involves applying enough pressure as you run your hand or hands firmly over the body contours to bend back the fingers slightly. Pressure is always applied on the push-away movement, but gentle contact is maintained also on the draw-back. Whole hands can be used or just thumbs and fingers.

b. *Superficial stroking*, sometimes called *efflourage*, is complementary to deep massage, which it often follows. It should be continuous and light, one hand following the other to keep up a constant body contact. Its action is quick and relaxing but should not be too prolonged, otherwise it will seem like a friction, or become tickly or irritating.

Kneading

This gentle wringing or squeezing technique is applied to large muscle groups that are gently lifted, usually with both hands, and gently but rhythmically squeezed and wobbled. The skilled masseur will glide his hands from one muscle group to another, keeping constant body contact while kneading. Too drastic kneading is unnecessary and ineffective. What is more, it is liable to produce bruising – particularly in the fair-skinned.

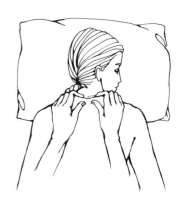

Skin rolling

This is to loose areas of skin – say, on the upper arm and abdomen – and is to skin what kneading is to muscles.

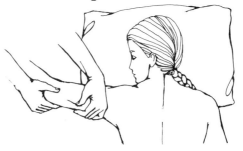

Friction

In massage terms friction is multiple deep pressure massage given by the tips of the fingers pressed well into the tissues and usually rotated in a 3-inch (7.5-cm) circle for about three minutes.

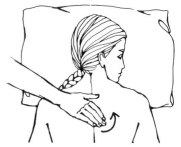

A SIMPLE RELAXING MASSAGE ROUTINE

This relaxing massage routine works on a head-to-toe basis and should take about 15–20 minutes to complete.

1. *Head and neck*

a. Stand behind partner and, using thumb or fingers, *deep stroke* forehead, face, nose and sides of neck. (The neck is best massaged by firm strokes down from the angle of the jaw to the root of the neck.)

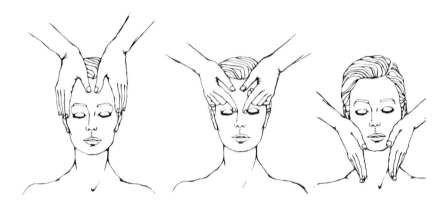

b. Then *superficial stroke* the same areas for about a tenth of the time you spent in deep stroking. Should there be tension in the jaw a *friction* over the joint of the jaw (in front of the ear) could be useful (see right).

How do you know if your massage is succeeding? First the frown lines or set-smile tension marks disappear from the face, and second there is a tendency for the mouth to open slightly.

2. Upper limbs

The giver masseur stands or kneels by the taker's right side as he or she lies on back on a couch or on the floor.

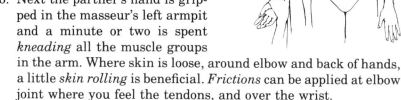

a. With the left hand the giver holds partner's right wrist away from the body and gives 10 *deep strokes* with the right hand from wrist to shoulder (up the inner side of the arm). Repeat on other arm.

b. Next the partner's hand is gripped in the masseur's left armpit and a minute or two is spent *kneading* all the muscle groups in the arm. Where skin is loose, around elbow and back of hands, a little *skin rolling* is beneficial. *Frictions* can be applied at elbow joint where you feel the tendons, and over the wrist.

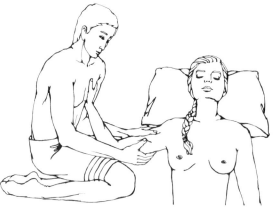

c. Finally, take your partner's outstretched palm and start *superficial stroking* from tips of fingers up into the hand, then into the forearm and up to the armpit. One hand should follow the other up the arm. Repeat for outside surface of arm starting with the back of the fingers and hand.

3. Legs

Again start with partner lying on his or her back with giver kneeling or standing at feet.

a. Use both hands to grip the foot, then *deep stroke* the whole of the limb from foot upwards. Repeat slowly four or five times.

b. Moving yourself slightly to one side, *knead* the large floppy deep muscles on the front of thighs.

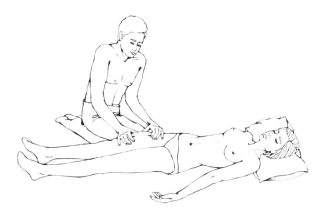

c. Follow this with *friction* at ankle and at sides of knees.

d. Repeat whole procedure on other leg. Then give five *superficial strokes* to each leg in turn.

e. Then get your partner to lie on his or her tummy and repeat the whole procedure on the backs of the legs.

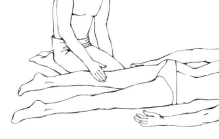

f. Finally, extend the *superficial stroking* to the whole of the back right up to the shoulders.

4. Back

a. Next, using one hand to reinforce the action of the other, *deep stroke* muscles of buttocks. These need to be moved passively by short deep stroking movements which have to take effect through the layer of buttock fat. Repeat five times. (This layer of fat is much thicker in women than in men.)

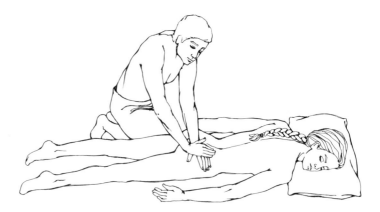

b. Less penetrating *deep stroking* of the lumbar muscles that run up from the buttocks to the waist follows. Both of these major areas need deep stroking. Again four or five good actions are necessary on each side.

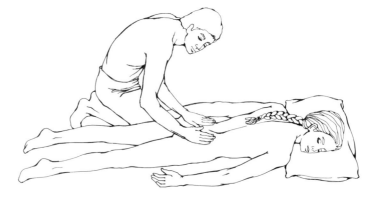

c. Next move your attention to the shoulder blades which should be rocked by *deep stroking* five times on each side, each stroke attempting to get a little more movement of the shoulder blade than the previous one.

d. Finally, *deep stroke* the big shoulder-lifting muscles (deltoids) up towards the nape of the neck, gliding into the large bunches of neck muscles as you leave the shoulder muscles.

e. Then commence the *lightest superficial stroking* of the whole of the back area before asking your partner to turn over and lie on his or her back. If the taker wishes it, continue the superficial stroking technique to the abdomen, breast and chest area before starting the next part of the programme.

Muscle relaxation component
First session

1. PENDULUM BREATHING

If you enter a relaxation programme here, without reading the section in the 10-day plan that seems most relevant to you, then you may be at a bit of a disadvantage. It is quite possible to learn the relaxation response with a friend, but both of you should first of all read pages 31 to 35 on pendulum breathing and practise this together for half an hour or so on two or three occasions before progressing any further.

a. The 'giver' continues in the role of relaxation tutor rather than masseur. It is important for the tutor to say to his partner something along the following lines: 'Although I am going to help you to relax, you are the one who got yourself tensed up in this way. These are *your* muscles and *you* are going to relax them. I've given you a massage to show you that I am involved in trying to help you. Now it's up to you to learn to relax, and it's an active not a passive process.'

b. While saying this arrange your partner on a firm couch, making sure that he or she is lying comfortably on the back with a pillow or cushion under the head. Constricting clothes should have been abandoned and the legs should be rotated outwards and parted slightly, the feet pointing about 45° away from the vertical. Knees are slightly flexed (bent). Arms should be by the side with the elbow joint about 6 inches (15 cms) away from the body, and the palms should rest on the outer thighs. Encourage your partner to wriggle comfortable. Take up the relaxation position yourself.

c. Establish pendulum breathing. Now no more wriggling or fidgeting is the rule. At this stage it is a good idea to say that initially strange itchings occur and that the face often becomes sensitive to out of place hair and so on. Stress that these are good signs: the body is really itching to relax. Practise pendulum breathing together for five minutes before you start the next part of the programme.

2. THE DIFFERENCE BETWEEN A TENSE AND A RELAXED MUSCLE

The next part of the programme for first-timers is to learn to recognize the difference between a tensed and a relaxed muscle. This has already been explained in the 10-day programme (pages 22 to 26 in particular).

a. Take your partner's right wrist in your hand and hold the arm out straight. Then tell your partner to *try* bending it up at the elbow. Ask where the stress or strain is felt. Always the partner will say 'where you are holding me' or 'where my arm is levering itself against the couch'. Then you must feel the biceps muscle of her right arm with your other hand. 'This is where the real tension is,' you tell her. Tell her to stay with this feeling for half a minute or so, and then relax her arm, feeling her muscle again and telling her to remember the difference in this feeling. Repeat this five times – it is a most important preliminary exercise for you both.

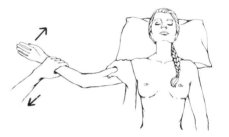

b. Repeat the procedure again with the triceps group of muscles at the back of the arm. These are best put into strong tension by you restraining your partner's bent arm (at the elbow) against your resistance. In other words she is trying to straighten her arm, but you won't let her. Do this five times, relaxing the muscles between each tension session, and encourage her to keep feeling the difference.

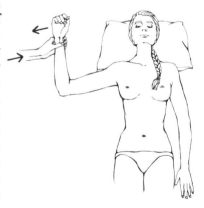

c. Having learned 'the difference' tell her to lie still and practise pendulum breathing while enjoying the difference. It is important to stress to your partner that this first lesson is very important. So important that it is worth repeating several times in an attempt to cultivate the new experience of feeling a muscle group in relaxation. At least five to 10 minutes of pendulum breathing completes the first lesson.

Some couples will want to reverse roles at this point. Others postpone this for some hours or do it the next day.

Second session

The second session starts with the whole body massage. Afterwards the giving partner moves into the second part of the relaxation teach-in.

The giver states what he is going to do thus: 'I want you now to start to switch your arms to "relax" at will – *not* by first feeling tense so that you can subsequently relax. You are going to switch your muscles to relax. Let them feel heavy, and when you have mastered this just nod to me and I will check.'

Pendulum breathing is now started and after 10 breaths the giver says, 'I'm waiting for the signal' (words from the taker are best not encouraged as they tend to start conversations). Once the signal is given the giver checks for the wobbly feel of the relaxed muscle. To start with this may only be a partial wobbliness, in which case the giving partner says, 'Let it go, let it go heavy – carry on with your breathing – in breathing into out – I want no pauses, keep the sounds the same.' Eventually the muscles, first one group, then the other, will relax. (It is usual for right handed people to find it harder to relax this right hand side than the left. For this reason in the relaxation teach-in the giver starts with the opposite side to the handedness of the body.)

Once the relaxed state of the arms is reached, both partners lie relaxed together and practise pendulum breathing for 10 minutes.

Third session

Once again the giver, after full body massage, moves into muscle relaxation exercises by extending the programme. Quickly run through Session Two. Don't try to compress it into too short a time for your partner (and you) will still be tension-prone and not able to relax quickly.

After the desired arm relaxation is complete move on to legs. If upper limb relaxation is still difficult, keep with Session Two for the whole of the time and proceed no further for a while. Don't despair if there is a 'stick' situation here, and don't try to move on further. Given patience and perseverance the lesson will be learned. Of course once the taker becomes the giver the course may proceed more swiftly. Few people learn the relaxation response at any special given rate.

LEGS

If Session Three is to involve the legs it is best to start with the calf muscles once pendulum breathing is established. If leg relaxation is not learned in Session Three, it should be preceded by a full massage in Session Four.

The leg muscles are more difficult to relax than the arms because as well as having a locomotor function involved in walking and running, they also have a proprioceptive function (see pages 22 to 23) which involves them in balance and standing still. The giver must say 'tense your calf muscles' and then 'relax them' so that the wobbly feel is appreciated by the giver. Once the fully developed wobble is present — maybe after several admonitions to 'relax more, they are still tight' — the taker may say that his or her muscles feel 'creepy', or 'like worms wriggling'. This sensation is due to certain areas in the calf muscle contracting spontaneously. The giver may actually be able to see these individual discharges of tension as small areas flick unconsciously into action.

Once calf muscles are well and truly relaxed the taker should stay with the feeling of the relaxed muscle for two or three minutes. Then move on to learn first how to relax the huge muscle on the front of the thigh (the quadriceps), and afterwards the hamstring muscles at the back of the thigh.

To relax these enormous groups of muscles it is easiest to start by half flexing the leg (the giver supports it with one hand while the other hand gently feels the muscles with his fingertips). Having

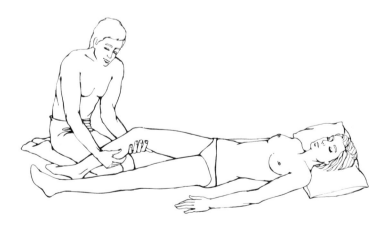

already learned how to relax the calf muscles it is relatively easy to relax these large groups on both sides of the thigh.

Finally switch roles, making sure to 'pick up' your partner at the same stage. Finish with pendulum breathing together.

Session four (or five)

Always start a new day with massage and now run through arm and leg relaxation. Once things are progressing smoothly and you gain confidence try extending relaxation to the large muscle that elevates the arm (the deltoid), the muscles under the breasts (the pectorals), and the muscles at the back of the neck. It is easy to identify these (in advance, by getting them to tense up). But don't introduce this tension phase into your new advanced relaxation programme. Do not be upset if you experience only partial success with these muscles. They are difficult to relax consciously and it is not worth while feeling a failure over not doing too well with them. It is easy to obtain the relaxation response without gaining total mastery over every muscle group – in fact spontaneous relaxation will occur in due course often when you least expect it.

Reverse roles as before, and finish with another pendulum breathing session.

Last session

Just how well relaxing with a friend has gone and how successfully you have worked yourself into it depends on many things, not least of which is how friendly you are with your partner. The relationship between the professional masseur and the customer is a pretty cold clinical one in many cases. But in our concept of mutual relaxation it is often possible to introduce a degree of intimate feeling that is rewarding in many ways. (Readers familiar with behavioural techniques in sex therapy will note similarities with 'sensate focus' in the way that I have designated the giver and the taker roles. This is not to imply that relaxing with a friend is anything in the nature of a sexual experience, merely a mutually acceptable sensual one in which sensible and agreed limits may be reasonably defined, if necessary, before the first session takes place.)

On the final day of the 'relax with a friend' programme, after the massage session and a general relaxation tour of the body, it may be worthwhile to explore face relaxation to complete the course.

If headaches have been a problem it is a good idea to find the eyebrow-moving muscles and gently persuade these to relax. Excessive tension in eye muscles may be involved with headaches too and the giver can put the eye muscles to strain by asking the taker to look carefully at something held about 6 inches (15 cms) in front of the nose, and then to stare into the distance. 'As you do this you can feel your eyes plop deep into their sockets' is a good phrase with which to coach the taker as this exercise proceeds. Continue for about half a minute.

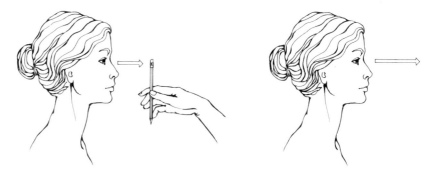

Finally the giver can summarize the whole question of relaxation learning by restating something said spontaneously by one relaxation taker in training. 'If I try to relax – I just can't. But if I first relax my arms, then my shoulders, my legs, the muscles in my head and neck one after another it comes quite easily. I can do it so quickly that the whole process only occupies a second or two, but I have to go at it in sequence.' Such a state of affairs can be yours for the asking. All you have to do is to take the time to learn.

CHAPTER 10

The popular image of faith healers tends to be a rather tarnished one, yet it is repeatedly being demonstrated that dramatic successes in the healing of many problems – both of physical and psychological disease – often follow when a patient submits, or surrenders himself, to a new faith. Cynics may say that if vast numbers of ordinarily intelligent men and women succumb to the foibles of commercially-minded quacks and rogues, then it is up to the doctors to tell them that they have been duped and fooled. But because the perpetrators of the 'cures' may have been shown to be, if not exploitative rogues and crooks, then empiricists, there is something intrinsically phoney about the cures themselves. Such an argument is often fallacious. A criminally insane surgeon could, for instance, carry out an efficient appendectomy operation and save a patient's life. In other words, the nature of the cure need have nothing to do with the personality, morals, or ideas of the healer. Rather, it is to do with what the healer *does* to his patient.

When cures follow a pattern that is at loggerheads with the tenets and beliefs of orthodoxy, it is common to look on them as being dubious 'faith cures', and much has been written on this subject from both sides of the medical blanket. An unprejudiced examination of faith cures shows us that faith, as such, is a powerful thing when it is firmly *in control* of a situation. Another factor intrinsic in such cures is the generation in one form or another of the relaxation response.

Meditation is the cornerstone of many religions and cults, for example in Zen Buddhism. Primarily designed by religion to benefit the soul, it is also excellent stuff for the body. In these days straightforward meditation rather than prayer is a feature of Oriental religions. But the Retreat has always had its place in the Church of Rome and is becoming popular in other religious persuasions too. Often, of course, the mantra has a different name, and the type of breathing learned in the 10-day plan may be more related to the canticle than the pendulum.

In recent years a new approach by the Occident to the Orient has been tentatively made in which the principles we have been concerning ourselves with in this book are more directly used.

Transcendental meditation

Transcendental meditation, or T. M., is defined by its enthusiasts as 'A technique which allows the mind to settle down to a less excited state – the person experiences quieter and quieter levels of thinking until he or she arrives at a state of complete mental stillness. Once this state has been attained the attention has transcended or gone beyond the everyday levels of thought.' T. M. is followed closely by an experience of body relaxation 'in which the subject does not sleep, is fully conscious' and, it is even claimed, experiences an 'inner wakefulness'.

Of all the more recent popular cults (the T. M. hierarchy stresses that it is not a religion), transcendental meditation holds pride of place for evangelism – its recruits worldwide number in excess of two million. The background of T. M. is suitably mystical and its founder is the Maharishi Mahesh Yogi. When a student at Allahabad University, the Maharishi fell under the spell of a venerable sage, it is claimed, and after two years of solitary cave dwelling went forth like Moses with his 20th-century 'tablets' to preach a new and enormously successful gospel.

In many cults there is a tendency towards poweful elitism. In T. M. this process is acknowledged, and a suitable hierarchy has developed. You cannot learn T. M., they say, from a book and so novices have to make an early financial commitment to their teachers, which is incidentally in no way a pittance. Happily the basic instruction or initiation is reasonably brief and can be taught at a course of four lessons over four days, beating hands down the detailed techniques described in this book in terms of time alone! Once initiated into the cult, to obtain permanent benefit 20 minutes' practice twice a day is mandatory. Basically T. M. relies heavily on a personally prescribed mantra and the relaxation response.

How effective is T. M.? The British Association for the Medical Application of Transcendental Meditation claims it reduces high blood pressure, improves the heart's function and reduces anxiety. As such it provides roughly the same advantages as does any one of the relaxation techniques outlined in the 10-day programme. It is also claimed to strengthen the immune system. Until comparatively recently such claims would have received scant attention from the world of medicine. Today, however, it has been proved, both experimentally and clinically, that undue stimulation of the stress hormones undoubtedly reduces resistance to infection, and so once again the health-giving side effects of all types of relaxation therapy are underlined. (See Chapter 13, page 178.)

Dr William A. R. Thompson, whose book *Faiths That Heal* provided invaluable research material for the preparation of this chapter, has pointed out an interesting effect of T. M. – namely its power as a socializing force in a community. The Maharishi International College in Britain is situated in Tonbridge, Kent. By the time T. M. had achieved a one per cent penetration into the pattern of living of those living within the jurisdiction of the Chief

Constable of Kent, the crime rate had fallen by 17 per cent. A similar phenomenon occurred in a community in the USA.

Yoga

I have borrowed techniques from yoga for the basic relaxation course. Perhaps to repay that secular theft from an established and venerated religion would not be out of place now.

Yoga is an integral part of Hinduism, its very name deriving from the 'yoke' that binds two together. The two in this case are the individual self and the universal self. Hinduism, like most Oriental religions, is permeated with sub-cults and disciplines, the apparent eccentricities of which have led to many misunderstandings as to its fundamental nature. The most straightforward (from our point of view) components of Hindu yoga are *asana*, with its concentration on physical postures, and *pranayama*, which involves controlled breathing similar to the pendulum breathing we have used so extensively. Yoga relaxation or meditation works on an easily recognizable principle which may be stated thus. If you control one automatic (autonomic) body mechanism – say, breathing – then other similarly automatically- (autonomically) controlled body functions will also become capable of control – for example, the level of the blood pressure, the heart rate, the activity of the digestive system, and so on.

The Hindu religion also has some very important things to say on the loss of peace of mind that is associated with many psychosomatic conditions. It directs its disciples to gain insight into the nature of the self and its relation to its environment, and to learn to rebuild loss of self esteem. It warns against the folly of becoming too bound, or attached, to persons, systems and objects within the world, and warns of the feelings of hatred that can spring so easily from a lack of gratification received from such persons, systems or objects.

Having mastered the relaxation response's facility for restoring the body, the Hindu then moves on towards achieving *samocha*, which may be thought of as a state of constant and deep peace experienced against a backdrop of relaxed body functioning and an acceptable everyday life.

Unfortunately yoga is associated with as many penny-catching cults as any other of the healing faiths. The fact that your local 'yoga class' may be held in a church hall or local community centre is no guarantee of its authenticity, or even that it may help you with self mastery. If, however, you can seek out and feel happy with a good teacher then yoga relaxation and Hindu principles should bring you health and a sense of well-being.

Zen

Zen is to Buddhism what yoga is to Hinduism. Buddha, the enlightened one, struggled long and apparently hard to attain his enlightenment under the *bodhi* tree at Buddh Gaya. His story, and that of his faith, is an interesting one, born from a disenchantment with his own religion, Hinduism. It contains an episode in the life of Buddha that is common to many religions. Son of a minor Rajah in Nepal, Buddha married a local princess and led a sheltered life. This is said to have been so because his father had heard from a soothsayer that his son would renounce the world. One day when out in the country he came for the first time among the poor and needy. Indeed, he met for the first time an old decrepit and sick man, and viewed a corpse. Such was his devastation when confronted with this experience of human mortality that Buddha forsook the world and went out alone to seek the meaning of life. Eventually he founded Buddhism.

When dying as an old man of 80, Buddha's last words to his disciples were reminiscent of those uttered elsewhere in the history of religion, and one would think that they might seem unlikely to inspire the uninitiated: 'Behold now brethren, decay is inherent in all component things! Work out your salvation with diligence! Be a light unto yourselves, for there is no other light.'

One of the things that Buddha tried to lose from his Hindu background in his search for truth was the Hindu emphasis on mystic trance. Nevertheless, his enlightenment and illumination came to him in a state of 'abstraction' (the relaxation response). This arose from a new *rapport* with Nature in which he saw that only by a destruction of a craving for life itself could sorrow and anguish be extinguished and a personal quietude obtained.

When Buddha died the Buddhist faith developed along different paths in different countries. One such path led to the concept of Zen, which means contemplation. Zen, which disclaims the canonical books of the rest of Buddhism, inspired the inhabitants of Japan, a country which today is strong in Zen Buddhism.

Zen is a form of self-contemplation. Probably best-known apostle of Zen in the Western world was the late Judge Christmas Humphreys. In an attempt to explain Zen in a few words he was at pains to dissociate it from the classical 'meditation schools', which he felt gave the impression of severe passivity. Instead he stressed the strenuous nature of work in a Zen monastery necessary for the 'breaking down of the bars of the intellect so that the mind may be freed for the light of the Enlightenment'. Even the 'hours of meditation are intensely strenuous', Judge Humphreys emphasized.

Zen Buddhism is an intricate process, in which activity and a transcendental state known as *satori* are combined. In essence, *satori* is a formalized and carefully controlled form of breathing, and so we see once again the link between breath control (pendulum breathing) and the control of other physiological and emotional systems that are otherwise thought to be outside conscious control – or are part of the autonomic nervous system. Clearly, disciples of Zen experience the relaxation response, and with it, as Christmas Humphreys said, 'a sense of certainty, of serenity, of clarity, and of unity with Nature and the Universe abound' that is both intensely satisfying and therapeutic.

Hypnotism and relaxation

We tend to think of hypnotism as a fairly modern technique (its first major protagonist was Franz Mesmer [1734–1815]), and with reference to sleep or trance-like states rather than to relaxation. Such a concept is only partly true. Aesculapius, the god of physicians, often relieved the suffering of his patients by gentle stroking, and I showed in the 10-day plan how stroking techniques can, if practised together with breathing control, effectively produce a profound relaxation. Aesculapius' patients often passed into a trance-like state or sleep after his ministrations. And so even in the earliest days of medicine a bridge was built between relaxation and hypnosis.

Surprisingly perhaps, even the hypnotists – medical or lay – have difficulty in defining hypnosis. Many point out that hypnosis is an altered state of awareness, an altered consciousness. Most differentiate it from the state of altered consciousness that we call sleep. Some say that the hypnotic state appears to occur in creatures other than Man. Dr Stephen Black, who has examined the subject in some depth, stresses that it occurs as a 'result of constructive or rhythmic stimuli *usually* imparted by another'. The italics are mine and indicate the possibility of self hypnosis.

A suggestion that a link may exist between the powerful personal magnetism of the persuasive and impressive Billy Graham-type orator and hypnotism has been made, and this ties in well with the other characteristic of hypnotism that we have not as yet mentioned – the important phenomenon known as hypnotic suggestion.

Post hypnotic suggestion has never been explained scientifically. Within its compass probably lies an explanation for every spell and incantation of the sorcerer and witch-doctor too. And if we believe this then maybe every miracle and faith cure as well! The fact that we cannot explain it, however, does not mean we should be frightened of it or turn away from it. In all probability hypnosis is a means of gaining mastery over attention. Becoming oblivious to the outside world, by sitting quietly and attending only to a single stimulus – the hypnotist's voice, an image, an idol or an ikon even – produces the state. The exact method of trance-induction does not matter very much. We would do well to remember that Dr James Braid, who seems to have come from a particularly down-to-earth Scottish medical background, reintroduced hypnosis to a 19th-century audience by inviting a friend to stare at the top of a wine bottle. After three minutes the 'subject' fell into a deep 'sleep' identical to the mesmeric trance.

Traditionally it has been held that not everyone can be hypnotized, and by inference that those who are suitable subjects are somehow weak and easily controlled by others – especially by the hypnotist. Nothing could be further from the truth. To some extent such an image of the powerful *controlling* figure of the hypnotist has been fostered by the theatre and by the magician who has often added hypnotism as a sub-speciality to his professional conjuring expertise. Perhaps the truth lies in a concept that those individuals who have the greatest facility to concentrate their attention on a single matter and resist the mind's normal and constant wanderings are the most likely to be able to appreciate the various altered states of awareness and consciousness which include hypnosis and to some extent the therapy we appreciate and know as the relaxation response.

A voice from the past – Couéism

I would like to conclude this brief explanation of links that draw together the friendly, rather domestic, bliss of the relaxation response with the world of the near supernatural or religious ecstasy by remembering a friendly enough little character called Emile Coué. Coué was an impoverished apothecary from Troyes in France who found fame and fortune in the early days of this century by the realization of the powers of what came to be called auto-suggestion. For auto-suggestion we may substitute such words as faith, autogenics or even relaxation response.

Although today it would be hard to find many people with even the remotest idea of who Emile Coué was, in the 1920s his followers were thought to number millions. When he died in 1926 the event was of such international importance that it would now merit an instant radio and television newsflash. Coué was a considerable cult figure, and for those who used Couéism it was an aid to living of considerable substance. His message has been recalled and revamped today largely by the German neurologist J. H. Schultz, and seems similar to what has become called autogenics. (An autogenics component is present in many of the techniques outlined in the 10-day plan.)

Coué's beliefs were simple and his message was plain. He maintained that 'the unconscious self is the grand dictator of all our functions' and that self-distrust plays a large part in the genesis of all our ills. He believed that auto-suggestion was capable of curing the majority of the problems which our flesh is heir to. His system happily was as simple as his credo. Every morning on waking and every night before sleeping it was necessary to shut the eyes and repeat 20 times (while moving the lips and mechanically counting 20 knots on a string or tape between the fingers) the words: '*Every day in every respect I am getting better and better*'. The important thing was the degree of concentration and the confidence and faith with which this mantra was repeated. Enthusiasts claimed that only three per cent of participants in Couéism failed to respond – some quickly, some less so.

Coué believed his system worked by 'annihilating' the conscious mind, while the subconscious mind stayed awake, receptive, and could be spoken to. Although his method does not apply any breathing, stroking or touching techniques, it demonstrates that the relaxation response (which was surely the therapeutic factor in this rather strange little treatment) can cleary be stimulated in a wide variety of ways, some of which doubtless we are unaware of still. That it is possible to think one's way into a satisfactory relaxation response has been amply demonstrated with reference to biofeed-back, which I shall discuss in the next chapter.

CHAPTER 11

Relax with Biofeedback

If all roads are said to lead to Rome, then we might also claim that there are very many paths that can carry us along the way to the relaxation response. Perhaps the most scientific and modern of all the relaxation techniques is by means of biofeedback.

It has been known for some years that the relaxation response is associated with several physiological changes in the body. The breath rate is decreased, as is the heart rate, and the blood pressure falls. The whole of the sympathetic nervous system is dampened down, and this means that muscles relax and use less oxygen. The amount of sweat produced by our skin is significantly reduced, although this is not obvious in normal circumstances.

The phenomenon of sweat reduction is taken advantage of in most biofeedback techniques. Although it is not possible to measure small changes in sweat production itself, such changes bring about secondary changes in the skin's resistance to the passage of an electric current. In other words, the skin's resistance changes radically with the very small changes in sweating brought about by altering the level of the relaxation response. These electrical changes can be easily turned into an audio signal by means of an electrical device built into a biofeedback monitoring unit.

A typical setting for biofeedback in action is as follows. The subject lies on a firm couch in the relaxation response position detailed on page 12. He has two finger electrodes fitted which are connected with a relaxometer biofeedback monitoring unit. The audio unit is tuned so that a steady sound signal is broadcast.

The subject is then asked to start the pendulum-type breathing, and once this is accomplished he goes into his previously-taught muscle relaxation routine. Autogenic components may be introduced or a mantra evoked. As the relaxation response proceeds the note of the transmitter either changes or ceases altogether. A weekly half-hour routine with biofeedback over a period of three months is the usual treatment.

A biofeedback machine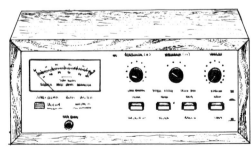

Doctors generally have been suitably impressed by biofeedback techniques. Carefully controlled trials have shown that blood pressure is so reduced by the intelligent use of biofeedback that medication often can be reduced or even eliminated. Similarly migraine attacks have been reduced in frequency and severity by means of this tecnique. Although biofeedback started medically as a non-drug remedy for high blood pressure, physicians have found it useful in controlling certain over-fast heart rate problems – the so-called tachycardias and heart arrhythmias.

As usual, once the medical profession obtains a new therapeutic toy they are not slow to devise uses for it. It is possible to combine biofeedback techniques with other techniques, for instance those that measure the electrical impulses which originate in the brain. Already it has been possible to identify an abundance of a special type of brain activity called alpha rhythm during relaxation procedures, which is associated with a feeling of tranquillity and calm. Similar applications of biofeedback have led to the discovery that relaxation response is useful in the control of epilepsy, and in one small clinical trial considerable reductions in the number of epileptic seizures experienced occurred in epileptics using biofeed-back relaxation response techniques.

One particular type of illness that does not respond very well to medication generally is periferal artery disease. This is a condition that often occurs in the legs, producing a variety of complaints including one called intermittent claudication in which the victim can only walk for a very limited period before he has to stop and rest. Angina is a similar periferal artery disease affecting the arteries of the heart (see Chapter 13).

The possibility of using biofeedback systems for altering blood flow is receiving attention and could prove useful.

A further modification of the biofeedback technique involves changes in skin temperature rather than skin electricity. A machine has been developed that uses this thermal measurement, and subjects can be trained by biofeedback means and the relaxation response to increase the temperature of their hands and limbs. This can be a very useful facility in the well-known cold illnesses, notably Reynaud's disease and chilblains. One type of migraine is characterized by cold hands occurring during an attack, and this particular problem can be alleviated by means of biofeedback training.

To what extent should we incorporate biofeedback into our mastery of the relaxation response? Probably not at all unless we are rich or enthusiastic enough to buy a biofeedback system for home use and learn how to use it to our advantage. There is, however, a biofeedback research society, and in hospitals and clinics in certain parts of the world biofeedback is very popular – notably in the United States where asthma, tension headaches, speech therapy, muscle tics and spasms, drug and alcohol habituation and epilepsy are commonly combated by using biofeedback techniques. In some centres gastrointestinal problems, including hiatus hernia and incontinence, are also being helped by biofeedback techniques.

Doubtless the hospital and clinic setting can use biofeedback as a useful therapeutic tool in many ways. But the relaxation response can be mastered easily in most cases by using the techniques we have described and without the need of such electronic hardware.

CHAPTER 12

We spend about a third of our life asleep and yet very little research has been directed towards solving the main sleep disorder – that of insomnia. Insomnia even lacks a precise definition. Of course insomniacs know what *they* mean by insomnia – it's a lack of sleep! And yet if we take such an insomniac into a sleep laboratory for a few nights, the electronic devices that subsequently monitor his sleep will usually show that he sleeps very nearly as much as 'good sleepers', as far as his total length of time asleep is concerned anyway.

How come, therefore, that whenever a survey is conducted into sleep it shows that roughly a fifth of the population complains of insomnia? Nobody knows for sure, and perhaps until more research is undertaken on the symptom of sleeplessness our knowledge will remain mainly anecdotal. But if you ask your friends what they mean by insomnia you will get several different answers. Most will say that it is a difficulty in *getting* to sleep. Others will say it is waking up too early or waking up too frequently in the night, and some will say it is just poor sleep and that they hanker after 'a really good night's rest'.

This last attitude is understandable. Sleep gives an opportunity for regeneration and repair of all our tissues, including the brain and muscles. The washed-out feeling after poor sleep is a very real one. During wakefulness, the rate of tissue breakdown in the body exceeds that of repair. In sleep, because of a reduction of energy demands and a different hormone patterning, the rate of renewal exceeds that of tissue breakdown. Experts in sleep, who base their findings on scientific data rather than the symptoms of their patients, are at pains to point out that although insomniacs sleep almost as long as their 'good sleeper' controls in the laboratory (and probably at home too), the *quality* of their sleep is deficient, and so the restorative nature of their sleep is not as good as it should be.

This is no informed guess of the sleep researchers. The electrical brainwaves that can accurately monitor sleep and wakefulness and tot up the sum total of sleep with a high degree of accuracy, show very little difference between the insomniac and the good sleeper. But when other tests are carried out, quite pronounced variations between the bad sleepers and the rest can be measured. The former have higher body temperatures and higher oxygen consumption during the night, and more stress hormones (corticosteroids) circulate through their system.

The sleeping pill routine danger

The instant refuge of the insomniac is, naturally enough, the sleeping pill. An incredible number of insomniacs have built a sleeping pill routine into their way of life, and would no more think of going to bed without their chemical sedative than without their pyjamas. Middle-aged women are especially dependent on the nightly sleeping drug, and most of us will take a sleeping pill occasionally.

A belief has been fostered in the minds of doctors – and their patients – that we have in our possession today drugs that do one thing and one thing only, and that is to promote good sound sleep at the drop of a hat. Unfortunately such a drug is still a pharmacological pipe dream. The drugs that exist to promote sleep are virtually identical to those used to promote a relief from anxiety, and all have built-in snags to them.

All drugs are basically dealt with by the body in one of two ways. Some are excreted unchanged in the urine, in the breath and by the bowel. Others, including sleeping pills, are broken down (metabolized) by the liver and similarly excreted. To carry out the latter function the liver produces certain detoxifying substances (enzymes) – which is just as well, for if it did not the drugs would kill us very rapidly. Once produced by the liver these enzymes are made in ever-increasing quantities to instantly 'mop up' fresh input of drug. This has a two-fold effect as far as sleeping pills or any other anxiety-reducing sedative drugs are concerned. First of all, to reach a much-wanted sleep-inducing degree of sedation an ever-increasing dose of the drug is necessary, and so there is a natural tendency to increase drug dosage. This in turn produces more detoxifying enzymes.

More important, however, is a second effect. Not only do the liver enzymes mop up the sedative more quickly, but they seem to promote a state of affairs characterized by an *increase* in anxiety and general twitchiness. Such an effect is seen in sharper focus in the withdrawal symptoms of the major addictive drugs, like heroin (when it is known as 'cold turkey'). The exact mechanism is unknown, but in all probability the liver enzymes which which have been produced to scour the system for potentially poisonous sedative drugs also have a similar mopping-up effect on the body's own naturally-produced anti-anxiety substances (including the little-known hormones that mediate in the relaxation response).

Unfortunately for the insomniac this adds up to one conclusion. By and large, and except in rather precisely defined circumstances, sleeping pills are disappointing therapeutically despite their widespread prescription.

THE GOOD, THE BAD AND THE INDIFFERENT

Modern sleeping pills of the benzodiazepine type are to some extent better than the older barbiturates, in that suicidal and accidental overdose are uncommon. Increasingly, however, people are becoming aware that all the benzodiazepines are not alike. Some persist in the tissues much longer than others, and some involve larger doses than others before they produce the effect that is desired. Yet another complication is that many of the drugs form breakdown products within the body that are very slowly eliminated. The drug flurazepam is characterized by its persistence in the system, to the extent that it accumulates in the tissues until it reaches a plateau in seven to 14 days. No wonder its takers so often feel strange in the daytime when on this sleeping pill.

Some of the benzodiazepines, especially flurazepam, diazepam and nitrazepam, have long 'half-lives' (the time between taking the drug and half of it being eliminated from the body). When this happens large amounts persist in the tissues next day and uncharacteristic behaviour on the part of the taker – for instance shoplifting or aggression may occur, and minor crime may be committed.

There are of course extremely short-acting benzodiazepines, for example triazolam with its half-life of only three hours. When this was introduced doctors felt that here at last was the ideal sleeping pill. Alas, due to the rebound phenomenon (see page 158) such a quickly-eliminated drug is ineffective in sustaining sleep and the taker often wakes up early in the morning awash with rebound anxiety.

One well-known sleep research authority suggests the best compromise is a drug with a half-life of about ten hours. Lormetazepam is such a drug. This, if taken, at 11 p.m. allows for a small amount to be present on waking – hopefully just enough to avoid a sharp daytime rebound of anxiety.

All the drugs I have so far mentioned are only available on a doctor's prescription. There are also available several over-the-counter sleeping pills, but few are very effective. An exception is promethazine (Phenergan) which is available in several strengths and as an elixir. It belongs to the class of drugs designated as antihistamine, and is an anti-allergic remedy with a sedative action. Like many antihistamines it does have a considerable sedative and prolonged action in most people, although in a few it has, paradoxically, the opposite effect.

WHEN NOT TO TAKE SLEEPING PILLS

It seems hardly sensible to take sleeping pills at all when so many sleep problems can be solved by relaxation methods. Those who *do* take sleeping pills, however, should see them as temporary expedients, and a clear goal for stopping them should always be envisaged.

Bronchitics and patients with emphysema should not take sleeping pills at all, because the drugs are always liable to depress their breathing centres. The elderly should not take sleeping pills either. Old people eliminate all drugs less effectively than the young. In many cases elderly people who seem confused are confused because they are battling their way through an 'azepam fog' at times when they should be alert. The elderly too may be unsteady on their feet, and the part that sedative drugs play in causing the horror of severe fractures in the elderly has never been accurately sought out. It is, in all probability, quite considerable.

HOW BEST TO HELP WITH INSOMNIA?

Better by far than dependence on drugs is for the insomniac first to learn the relaxation response, and then to learn, in the simple way outlined in the next three pages, how to use the relaxation response to promote easy sound sleep unhampered by addictive chemicals of any sort.

It is important to look at exactly where the insomniac *is* with reference to his very private world of insomnia. If, as is so often the case, he is taking sleeping pills he will have to face going through what is called *the rebound.* Starting to use a hypnotic drug helps sleep to come and makes sleep less broken; stopping a hypnotic drug makes sleep harder to come by and makes it more broken. As all hypnotic drugs also reduce anxiety, a similar rebound phenomenon occurs here too. Some popular sleeping pills have rather long actions – up to seven or eight hours – and enough sedative action remains in the system during the following day to allay anxiety until the next dose is taken at night. In many ways the sleeping pill habitué is in the same trap as the heavy drinker, whose evening dose of alcohol becomes fully metabolized by the morning and causes him to face either a painful degree of anxiety then – or another large whisky to 'settle his nerves'.

It is possible for medical help to modify the rebound phenomenon and make it less worrying and traumatic. Always, however, it has to be faced before more natural sleep and anxiety-reducing therapy can put the insomniac or the tension-ridden victim back on the right road.

How to programme yourself for sleep

Better sleep both for those who have battled their way through the rebound phenomenon and for the luckier insomniac who has not yet succumbed to the sleeping pill 'confidence trick', is based on the following general principles. What can be offered in the way of using the relaxation response is dealt with later.

First, the biological rhythm of natural sleep must be strengthened if better sleep is desired. We all tend to fall asleep if we are bored, immobile, and nicely warm without being hot. Often we fall asleep when we are short of sleep, that is unless we are excited or aroused. An important factor is the time when we are ready for sleep. The transcontinental traveller, particularly if he flies in the east to west direction, soon appreciates what sleep deprivation means, and often feels very odd indeed when he has to be awake when he should be asleep. Surprisingly often insomnia results from staying up an hour or so after one's normal bedtime – the time when sleep comes easily – for a natural biological rhythm can be by-passed quite easily and does not always return when we wish it to. Early nights are often very disappointing too when the early night is followed by an early waking.

Regular exercise, though not sudden night-time exertion such as late jogging or nocturnal dog walking, is good for sleep. It has been proved that open air exercise during the daytime makes sleep come on earlier and makes it last longer. The characteristic of the sleep is deeper in such circumstances and more growth hormone is released to restore the tissues. Nobody knows exactly why it should be so, but malted drinks such as Horlicks at night *do* make sleep more beneficial than do other bedtime drinks. Late feeding is bad for sleep, and so are coffee, tea, cigarettes and alcohol. However, provided the dose is kept the same, the alcohol nightcap of a large whisky or whisky and milk does help some people relax and get into the mood for sleep. But with alcohol there is always the tendency to increase the dose to get the much wanted (anticipated) effect because the body soon gets used to it. And therein lies the danger of using alcohol in this way.

One general practitioner has evolved his own code of advice for insomniacs, and his suggestions have a ring of authenticity about them that suggests he has tried them on himself and found them effective.

A DOCTOR'S PERSONAL SLEEP PRESCRIPTION

1. Go to bed when sleepy, but do not try to get more sleep by going to bed early.

2. Only read, eat or watch TV in bed if you know from past experience that such things help you get to sleep.

3. When you go to bed try to get all your muscles as relaxed as you can.

4. Do not think about getting to sleep or about the day's activities – try instead to dwell on pleasant places and activities. (The alarm should be set for the same waking time each morning.)

5. If pleasant thoughts do not come, then dwell on outside noises, traffic – anything monotonous will do.

6. If you do not go to sleep quite quickly, say in 10 to 15 minutes, get up instead of lying in bed fretting. Worrying about being awake is much worse than not sleeping. Instead, go into a different room and read or listen to the radio until sleepy. This 'quiet room', it is recommended, is worth setting up by insomniacs as a routine retreat. It should have a comfortable chair, adequate heating, blankets, a suitable reading light and a facility for making a drink. It should be a standby for the early wakers as well as for those who find it difficult to drop off. Once a sleepy feeling returns, the insomniac returns to bed and usually to sound sleep.

As far as item 3 on this list is concerned, the relaxation response can certainly help with sleep.

The following routine is very effective and differs from the relaxation response routines outlined in the 10-day plan, which are not designed to induce sleep. By now you know how best to relax or trigger the relaxation response. For insomnia you should devote yourself to a sleep-inducing procedure that uses some of the knowledge of self-hypnosis contained in Chapter 10.

SLEEP RELAXATION TECHNIQUE

1. After programming yourself for sleep lie in bed and work your way into a relaxed muscle state. (Particularly useful is Day One, Group 2 Routine 1 on page 24.)

2. Now switch to pendulum breathing (Day Two, pages 31 to 35) and breathe four regular in and out breaths. Then pause for a breath's duration (count 1, 2, 3, 4).

3. After this, repeat the process with only three in and out pendulum breaths and pause again for one breath's duration.

4. Reduce now to two breaths and pause, and then a single breath and pause.

The pendulum and pause seems to make all the difference between producing the relaxation response (in which sleep is neither desired or welcome) and a self-hypnotic condition in which sleep soon follows. This sleep-breathing technique can be used effectively by frequent wakers and those whose sleep is disturbed by other things – for example painful or irritable conditions, bladder problems, and so on. Early wakers (provided their doctor has excluded a psychiatric problem e.g. depression) can also benefit from this sleep relaxation technique.

How Stress Causes Illness

CHAPTER 13

Illnesses where relaxation can help

Up until now we have concentrated on using the relaxation response to improve the quality of our lives, to help us come to terms with anxiety, or to get away from tension. And so we have seen how relaxation helps us to sleep better, stops us from turning to the misery of drug addictions – to tranquillizers as well as to alcohol and nicotine – and helps us to cope with the common problems of living.

Dr Herbert Benson, who has done so much to popularize the relaxation response and show ways of obtaining its benefits, talks about the stress-induced diseases as being 'diseases with no symptoms'. This is true to some extent. Ideally, if we build the relaxation response into our lives early enough we may sometimes stop diseases at the stage when they have no symptoms.

For those who have the cardiac symptoms of the stress-related diseases, or at least have been diagnosed as sufferers, the following guide will prove helpful.

Blood pressure, angina and heart attack problems

Angina and heart attacks usually have a common denominator. A disease process in an artery or a group of arteries that supply the heart's own muscle (the *myocardium*) interferes with the supply of blood to that muscle. Muscles thus deprived of oxygen soon become flooded with *metabolites* – the breakdown 'afterburn' products of muscular activity. These in conjunction with lack of oxygen give cramp-like pain in any muscle group. When this cramp-like pain arises in the heart muscle we call it angina, from a Greek word meaning 'to throttle'. The angina victim does actually feel that he is being throttled – choked, you might say – by what is going on in his heart.

Heart attacks, or coronary thrombosis attacks, stem from a further progression of artery disease. The pain of angina, basically caused by a reduction in the bore of the artery, sometimes signals an alteration in the structure of the artery wall. Doctors call this process *atheroma*, and the patches of changed structure in the blood vessel wall are sometimes referred to as *atheromatous plaques* or patches. These alterations of the vessel wall are microscopic to start with. Gradually over the years they grow until they are visible to the naked eye. A constant and sustained higher than normal blood pressure helps them to progress. We know that constant and sustained stress and tension tend to produce a constant and sustained rise in blood pressure, and so the first major relationship between tension and disease is manifest.

But there is another bodily change brought about by stress. Strangely, perhaps, this is an entirely natural one. Stress is (in Nature) the body mobilizing itself for a natural situation. For instance there will be a biological advantage for the fighter, or the man who flees, if his wounds stop bleeding quickly. Wounds stop bleeding quickly if the blood clots easily, is rapidly coaguable in other words; stress alters blood so that it is rapidly coaguable.

An unfortunate situation is thus built into the system. Stress and tension are the 20th-century equivalent of 'fight and flight'. Only rarely are wounds inflicted and blood actually flow. But the stress-induced blood stickiness still occurs. And if arteries are also providing a suitable niche for blood to 'stick' in (the atheroma patch), then clotting (a coronary thrombosis) is liable to occur.

So we see there are two very obvious ways in which learning to relax can help to prevent a devastating disease which is liable to attack one man in three (and one woman in two) during middle age. Control of high blood pressure can stop the artery disease developing in the vessel walls to such an extent that an angina-producing patch can grow. Secondly, regular relaxation can coax the blood out of its high clotting tendency which produces the blood clot that forms coronary thrombosis.

WHEN TO START – HOW TO START

1. In youth
To prevent the high blood pressure that so often is the trigger factor which leads relentlessly to the flashpoint of a heart attack (and which may or may not be preceded by angina), the relaxation response grafted on to everyday life from early adult days onwards seems almost obligatory if continued good health is desired. In other words, our Group 1 novitiates who work through their 10-day course and sensibly build a regular relaxation time into their life will live longer and stay fitter than they would otherwise.

2. In early middle age
People in their 30s and 40s may seem to be perfectly fit, but they may, however, be suffering from the 'disease with no symptoms'. If their blood pressure is repeatedly checked (in a situation that discounts temporary and transient highs on the blood pressure scale) then some form of blood pressure lowering procedure will stop the inevitable process by which high blood pressure leads to angina or heart attacks.

It is always a doctor's responsibility accurately to tailor the treatment to fit the patient. Maybe drugs, lifestyle changes, and body weight adjustment will be necessary. In many cases if relaxation can be taught, either using Group 1 or Group 2 techniques, it will be possible to reduce blood pressure to normal levels. If long-term prophylactic medication is embarked upon prior to the relaxation response being taught, drug regimes with their inherent inconvenience and side effects can often be safely abandoned (under medical supervision) once the relaxation response is learned and built into the lifestyle.

3. Older people

Usually some organic changes will have occurred in the blood vessels or the heart (or both) with advancing years. In other words, the stage of a 'disease without symptoms' has passed. Often drug regimes will have been started to try to control symptoms and to restore more efficient function. Modern drug therapy has much to offer on this score. A suitable relaxation regime (Group 3) will be beneficial. Even in the presence of structural artery changes that, alas, relaxation will have difficulty in altering now, the battle is by no means lost. The relaxation response will still be able to alter the 'stickiness factor' of the blood, and during the period of relaxation the body uses less oxygen for its general wear and tear functions and thus leaves more for the heart to use in its often straitened circumstances. If someone in Group 3 is severely disabled by their illness they can omit altogether the physical components from the teaching method, or concentrate only on mastery of the relaxation response. A suitable regime is as follows:

TEACH YOURSELF TO RELAX REGIME FOR PEOPLE WITH BLOOD PRESSURE AND CARDIAC PROBLEMS OF AN ESTABLISHED NATURE

Day One

Start on Day Two of the 10-day course (page 31) and learn the essential pendulum breathing techniques. (Often it is an advantage to have someone to help such patients; the helper should read Chapter 9, Relax with a friend.)

Day Two

Follow the Group 3 Swedish hand friction instructions on page 43. Then repeat your pendulum breathing practice.

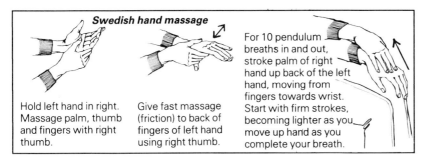

Swedish hand massage

Hold left hand in right. Massage palm, thumb and fingers with right thumb.

Give fast massage (friction) to back of fingers of left hand using right thumb.

For 10 pendulum breaths in and out, stroke palm of right hand up back of the left hand, moving from fingers towards wrist. Start with firm strokes, becoming lighter as you move up hand as you complete your breath.

Day Three

Turn to page 54 and carry out the Group 3 arm relaxation instructions, but leave section at end of Routine 1. Finish with 15 minutes' pendulum breathing.

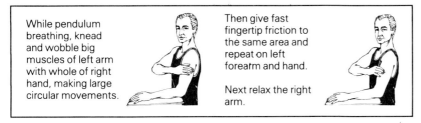

While pendulum breathing, knead and wobble big muscles of left arm with whole of right hand, making large circular movements.

Then give fast fingertip friction to the same area and repeat on left forearm and hand.

Next relax the right arm.

Day Four

Move to the Group 2 hand and arm exercises on pages 50 to 53. Finish with 15 minutes of pendulum breathing.

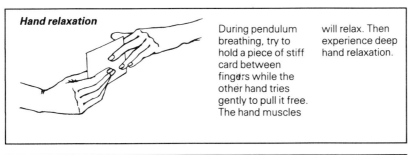

Hand relaxation

During pendulum breathing, try to hold a piece of stiff card between fingers while the other hand tries gently to pull it free. The hand muscles will relax. Then experience deep hand relaxation.

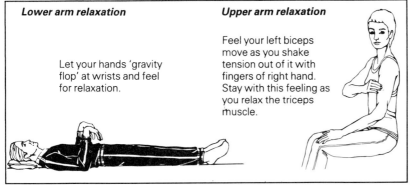

Lower arm relaxation

Let your hands 'gravity flop' at wrists and feel for relaxation.

Upper arm relaxation

Feel your left biceps move as you shake tension out of it with fingers of right hand. Stay with this feeling as you relax the triceps muscle.

Day Five

Practise pendulum breathing for 5 minutes, then do your Day Three arm relaxation exercises, followed by your Day Two Swedish hand exercises. Finish with 15 minutes' pendulum breathing.

Day Six

Follow the first four exercises for Group 3 on pages 67 to 68. Finish with 15 minutes' pendulum breathing.

Day Seven

Follow the first muscle relaxation session for 'Relax with a friend' (as a taker only), pages 139 to 141, and finish with pendulum breathing for 15 minutes. (If you are uncomfortable lying down get your giver to improvise as much as possible in a reclining position.)

Day Eight

Follow 'Relax with a friend' (as a taker only, and excluding the massage), page 141, second session. Finish with 15 minutes of pendulum breathing.

Day Nine

Follow 'Relax with a friend' (as a taker only, and excluding the massage), pages 141 to 142, third session. Finish with pendulum breathing for 15 minutes.

Day Ten

Make this a Conference Day to decide which sort of relaxation suits you best, most helps your symptoms, and reduces your pain and distress. A selected adventure into the fascinating world of relaxation should be built into your life two or three times a day. Check with your doctor in case your medications can be reduced or forgotten after a few weeks.

AFTER A CORONARY

Many a person first starts really to look at himself, or his lifestyle, *after* he has had his first coronary. He will want to know what the relaxation response can provide in the way of rehabilitation at this stage. To some extent the selected relaxation regime will be dictated by what the heart specialist has to say about the victim's cardiac fitness – that is, how well the heart now functions as a pump.

In many cases the heart remains virtually as fit as it was before the thrombosis. Often the heart specialist will establish that his patient would do well to get himself involved in a fairly athletic regime – possibly far more athletic a regime than had been built into his life for some years. If this is so it may be possible to pick up the 10-day relaxation course as a Group 1. If the cardiac reserve is good without being excellent, Group 2 is an ideal starting point, but if routine medication follows the heart attack, or if heart surgery is contemplated or has been undergone, Group 3 should be the preferred regime, despite age.

Often after an episode of coronary thrombosis spouses find themselves closer together in their feelings than they have been for some time. They may wish to learn the 'Relax with a friend' routine (Chapter 9), which in such cases can be a very good entrance to the health-giving citadel of the relaxation response. But whichever portal of entry is contemplated it can be stated emphatically that some positive health benefit will certainly follow.

THE DISABLED AND THE RELAXATION RESPONSE

Stress disease involving the heart and blood vessels all too often leave their victims severely disabled, and it is not only the arteries of the heart and the heart muscle itself that suffer. The blood vessels that supply the kidneys can be involved, and those organs suffer partial or complete failure. Stroke illness is another sequel to the combination of blood vessel disease and high blood pressure; in fact, a stroke is often the first signal that the 'disease without symptoms' is there – and has been there for several years, maybe for half a lifetime.

Just what can be done in individual circumstances varies enormously. The physiotherapist can, however, do much in the acute stage of these illnesses, and provided a degree of stability can be established teaching the relaxation response can be subsequently added to any treatment package. There is no condition that I have come across in the disabled and the very elderly which is not improved by the introduction of a first aid programme of relaxation training.

A simple relaxation technique

Perhaps the simplest example of a method of relaxation is the one advocated by Dr Herbert Benson and operated at the Beth Israel Hospital, Boston. It is a particularly useful technique for those who are disabled or ill.

1. Sit quietly and comfortably and close your eyes.

2. Consciously relax all your muscles starting at the feet and working up your body to your face. Concentrate on keeping them relaxed.

3. Breathe through your nose and be aware of the breathing process. After you breathe out say the word 'ONE' to yourself. Continue in the rhythm of breathe in, breathe out and say 'ONE'. Breathe in, breathe out, say 'ONE'.

4. Practise this breathing for 15 to 20 minutes. You may open your eyes to see the time, but do not use an alarm of any sort. When your relaxation programme is over sit quietly for several minutes. (Some people drop off to sleep for a few minutes after they have finished their breathing exercises.)

It is as well to remember that during such a short cut to the relaxation response it will be difficult to feel much benefit to start with. A deep level of relaxation will not occur at the beginning but this does not matter provided a totally passive attitude is maintained. Gradually the desired relaxation creeps in. To start with distracting thoughts will intrude. Do not try to chase them away or dwell on them or follow them up in any way – just dismiss them as best you can. The breathe in, breathe out, say 'ONE' recipe will help in this way.

It is advisable not to try to elicit the relaxation response within two hours of a meal as the desired degree of relaxation does not come easily to a full stomach (sleep is more likely to be induced). As with all methods of relaxation, a twice-a-day routine must be part of your new way of life.

How you know it's working

1. A sense of calm is experienced.

2. Some people experience a feeling of pleasure, well-being or even something approaching ecstasy.

3. Others get very little subjective experience, but their symptoms become less troublesome because their body has, for a while anyway, used up less oxygen, allowing other tissues to work just that little bit better.

A modification of this very simple type of relaxation response is to say a prayer or to recite a mantra (see Chapter 3) in time with the breathing pattern and omit the 'ONE' at the end of each controlled breath.

Chronic indigestion and peptic ulcer

A medical debate as to what really causes gastric ulcers has been running for years. Leaving the almost universal symptom of dyspepsia aside for the minute, it seems highly likely that the gastric and duodenal ulcer have a multiple causation. An ulcer is a lack of continuity of tissue – a hole in other words. If you knock some skin off your leg and it does not heal, you have an ulcer. In a way you can liken a peptic ulcer (the modern term that includes both gastric and duodenal ulcers) to a hole anywhere. All sorts of things can cause a hole in the rug in front of your fire – for instance a spark may make a burn hole in it; somebody's sharp stiletto heel may punch a hole in it; if you shut your dog in the room by accident he may scrape a hole in it, too. Holes in carpets are multifarious as far as their causation is concerned and so are peptic ulcers, and when such a hole is present developing symptoms of indigestion will occur.

It seems likely that all sorts of things produce small holes in the lining of the stomach. Something sharp such as a piece of pork crackling may graze your inside in the same way as you may graze or remove some skin from your knees by a minor accident. Of course these minor 'ulcers' soon heal, although the stomach is at special risk in some ways, as we shall see later. The air that surrounds most ulcers on our hands or shins does not interfere with healing. But your stomach always contains quantities of quite strong acid and powerful digestive enzymes that help you digest and utilize the food you eat. Exactly why the stomach and part of the duodenum do not automatically digest themselves all the time has always baffled doctors. But of course they do not. However, if acid levels are high a minor injury to the lining of these organs may well not heal very quickly. This acid theory has traditionally been put forward to explain why peptic ulceration occurs, but modern research suggests an entirely different basic causation, although gastric acid and intestinal enzymes are obviously implicated too.

In the 19th century a United States army surgeon called William Beaumont had a piece of luck with reference to one of his patients, a man called Alexis St Martin. This man suffered an abdominal wound which meant that there was an artificial opening of his stomach to the surface that would not heal (such an opening is called a fistula). Due to this disability it was possible to study the composition and volume of his gastric juices in varying circumstances from hour to hour. Dr Beaumont as a result gained early knowledge of the function of the stomach and the circumstances that altered this function. One of his findings was that if his patient was annoyed or angry his stomach did not empty itself as it should. In fact, it became overfull and acid-dyspepsia was experienced.

During the last few years research of a much more sophisticated nature has disclosed several other secrets of indigestion. Gradually a consensus of opinion has developed on how the gastrointestinal tract responds to emotions and to stress. Sudden emotional upsets or a toxic substance entering the stomach produce a quite sudden lack of tone in the stomach itself. The normal contractions that usually waft the contents of the organ gently along disappear. As a result the victim feels 'sick with apprehension', and indeed vomiting may occur.

If, however, someone experiences what might be described as a forced withdrawal from an emotionally charged situation, or if some sort of internal conflict occurs in which the natural response of aggression or fighting back is stifled for one reason or another, then an entirely different gastric reaction is noted. The stomach and the rest of the bowel becomes tense. Waves of contraction are very evident. A lot of excess gastric juice is produced which is also very strong and acid. If you look at a stomach (through a little tube called a gastroscope) at such times it looks very red and inflamed – hot and bothered (a bit like its owner).

Thus anxiety and stress have very definite effects on our insides generally. An overwhelming state of anxiety – seeing something very disgusting or offensive, the helpless feeling experienced when one suddenly realizes that something has been taken on that can't be handled – is followed, as mentioned previously, by a total stoppage of the gastrointestinal tract, and with this functional collapse the victim may vomit or develop diarrhoea.

A similar reaction is seen too in the passive person who is full of hatred, defiance or contempt. On the other hand, those whose lives are tinged with anger and resentment, whipped by hostility or threatened by anxiety, react by an over-activity of the stomach with hunger pains, dyspepsia and acid indigestion looming large in their symptom complexes.

The natural logic of such digestive troubles in terms of the function of the body under stress is easy enough to understand. The massive shut down of the system in which nausea, vomiting and sudden diarrhoea are experienced is evidence of the body getting ready to fight or flee. The system then wants all its blood to be available for the heart, the circulation and the muscles, with survival in mind.

When gastric over-action is in evidence, the physiology is rather more complex. In a way it appears to be related to subconscious hunger and the desire to be fed and cared for. From its earliest days a baby learns to associate fear, anger and anxiety with hunger. When he is hungry the baby is experiencing the fundamental life stimulus – the desire to be nurtured and to survivè. This being so, he also associates hunger with a feeling of being uncared for, being denied and rejected. He responds by expressing anger and primitive aggression in the only way he can, while all the time his little stomach is preparing itself for that moment that (hopefully) will soon arrive by means of an increased blood flow through the stomach and a higher gastric acid and digestive enzyme production. At this stage of anxious anticipation the inside of the stomach is potentially more fragile and may be easily damaged.

It is important to realize that all this is not some sort of physiological daydream of the scientist. It is backed up by solid evidence from a variety of sources. Whole populations in which sustained anxiety and tension is an outstanding component of their lifestyle suffer more dyspepsia, peptic ulcers and the complications of ulcers, such a perforations and haemorrhages, than do other less stressed communities.

The overall medical management of dyspepsia and peptic ulceration is not the subject of this book. Most simple isolated dyspepsias settle quickly and easily with the popular antacids sold at chemists; more troublesome ulcers, either suspected or proved, respond to more specific remedies, notably those that cut down on the amount of acid secreted by the stomach. Always it seems we have to pay for drastic alteration in the body's internal chemistry through effective drug treatment by the development of side effects, some of which are unpleasant, dangerous or difficult to bear. (The drug totally without side effects is often a drug which is totally ineffective.) Sometimes, and often due to reasons that defy accurate assessment, treatment by medicines is ineffective in the management of peptic ulcers. In such cases surgery can have a lot to offer.

Relaxation, carefully learned and carried out on a basis that builds it into the lifestyle, has a great deal to offer in the management of dyspepsia and its sequel if neglected, peptic ulceration (except in cases where mechanical problems or complications dictate surgery). Anyone who finds their life being dominated by their stomach, what they eat and what they do, would do themselves a vast service by learning what the relaxation response has to offer.

TROUBLESOME BOWELS

There seems no doubt that the gastrointestinal tract has suffered at the hands of civilization. In the previous section I explained the part that stress and the emotions play in the whole process of digestion and peptic ulceration. But the stomach, its attached duodenum and the small intestine, which are all concerned with digestion and absorption of food, are not the only organs to suffer from our modern patterns of living. The rest of the bowel does so as well.

One of the most interesting changes that civilization has brought to mankind is to alter his food. Even at the turn of this century a large proportion of the food we ate was natural food. Then with the age of the machine it became possible to refine and process food. Flour was made whiter and people thought, therefore, it was purer and better. Sugar was extracted from cane and beet and farm animals started to be fed by man rather than to forage for themselves. During the course of the 20th century food preservatives, additives, flavour improvers and so on evolved, which have added up to a state of unhealthy eating that is still only half suspected.

Perhaps the simplest and most obvious alteration to our diet has been brought about by over-refinement of grains. This in turn has led to a subsequent lack of bulk and roughage in the diet, which has produced several of the major bowel diseases today – notably constipation, colitis, the irritable bowel syndrome, and diverticulitis. Some would argue that large bowel cancer is also associated with our 20th-century self-imposed dietary modifications, for it is very rare in societies that eat more natural foodstuffs. There is no doubt at all that the reintroduction of more fibre into our food – if not by a back-to-natural-food movement, which often seems to be almost impossible today, then by fibre supplementation – is vitally necessary. In other words, by re-adding the bran we first of all so expensively removed from the natural grains we eat our health will improve. But this is not the whole story of troublesome bowels. Psychological factors have a big part to play in all bowel ailments, although this is seldom stressed today.

The large bowel reacts to psychological upset in a similar way as the stomach and small intestine. The type of person who reacts to psychological upset and tension by feeling depressed and apathetic usually develops constipation and suffers from the side effects of that constipation – piles, and so on. Those people who react to stress by feelings of repressed anger, hostility and frustration, tend to develop an over-active large bowel in which the frequent passage of poorly formed motions, excessive intestinal gas production and bloating of the intestine are common symptoms. Some sufferers seem to self-damage their bowel even more, possibly because stress hormones reduce the healthy viability of the mucous membrane of the bowel to normal intestinal organisms. They subsequently develop ulcerations and colitis, diverticulitis and other worrying large bowel diseases.

No-one would argue that the ultimate cause of colitis in its various forms is fully understood. We do know, however, that a gradual return to more healthy eating patterns, including eating more vegetable bulk and bran, pays enormous dividends in cases of the extremely common irritable bowel syndrome.

It is possible today to carry out experiments that accurately monitor the function of the colon and see how it reacts to suppressed anger and conditions of conflict. We can monitor its increased degree of contractability, and even watch its angry redness. Learning the simple process of muscular relaxation and controlled breathing quieten the automatic (autonomic) impulses that originate in the brain, thus persuading the internal organs not to over-react to the tension of modern life to such a degree. The relaxation response can enormously help the irritable and over-active bowels to behave more normally and quietly.

Stress and your skin

Dermatologists (skin specialists) would like to persuade us that the skin rather than the eye is the mirror of, if not our soul, then man's basic emotions. There is good reason for linking the skin and our emotions, for both the skin and the brain develop from the same cells in the developing embryo. A few years ago over 100 dermatologists were asked at a meeting if they found that psychological factors were important in the development of skin diseases. All but one answered in the affirmative.

This response does not mean that all skin diseases are brought about by excesses of stress and nervous tension. Developmental faults, chemical and physical factors, the influence of drugs and bacterial and nutritional problems are all background factors in skin disease. What does come to light, however, is that anxiety, stress and the skin are intimately linked. The automatic (autonomic) nerves of the skin originate in the same areas of the brain as are located the centres involved in the management of the relaxation response. Because these autonomic nerve fibres influence such important functions as skin temperature, sweating and hair erection, it would indeed be strange if skin problems and stress problems were not closely related.

If we look at the skin with special reference to the emotions and stress, the link is plainly seen. Blushing, flushing and sweating are common stress reactions known to us all. For the majority they are transient phenomena of no serious import. But if they occur too easily or are too long maintained, they result in an over-flushed skin (as seen in the skin disease *rosacea*) or an over-sweaty skin (giving the symptoms of *hyperhidrosis*). It also seems likely that too frequent stimulation of the skin's autonomics is involved in the production or maintenance of dermatitis, eczema and the condition known as pruritus. (Pruritus means, in Latin, 'to itch'. And so when you go to the doctor and complain of an itchy rash and he learnedly diagnoses pruritus he is really saying 'you itch' which isn't so very helpful.)

ITCHY SKIN

Itching is such a universal symptom in skin trouble that it deserves closer investigation. Itching is thought by neurologists to be a type of very low intensity pain produced by a minimal type of stimulus. In other words, something irritates you and you tend to get rid of it by a quick scratch. But there is another component to itching. Somewhere in the brain there is a centre which seems to prime the skin (itself a projection of the nervous system) to become over excitable – to over-react. If you watch closely the fingers of many people who appear on television, you will be surprised by how frequently they scratch themselves, betraying an often unsuspected degree of tension.

Looking at itching as a stress-related symptom is highly relevant for it occurs in the same ways and situations as do other stress symptoms. It is frequently time-related or situation-related. Suppressed anger or irritation can often be partially released by having a good scratch. Patients have been known to complain that whenever they feel angry and cannot express it normally, they get itchy all over. Even the expression 'irritating moments' tells us a lot about the relationship between itching and tension. A man who suffered greatly from eczema got better when his elderly mother was admitted to hospital, for she subconsciously irritated him. Some people will get urticaria (hives) when faced with a stress problem, an examination, a social event, an interview or even a holiday. Two well-known orthopaedic surgeons were so antagonistic to one another that if they met one would immediately break out in the itchy hand rash called pomphlyx and subsequently could not operate for several days. Needless to say, he went to elaborate means to avoid a chance encounter with his colleague!

ACNE

Next to itchy skin diseases acne is probably the most prevalent problem in dermatology. At first sight it would appear hard to relate pustular acne, with its nasty spots, and the emotions. But a link there is and a very strong one.

We know today that the fundamental problem in acne is a change in the physical characteristics of the sebum (skin grease) that is produced in the sebaceous glands. This sebum is a valuable protective to skin health in normal circumstances. An optimum degree of skin greasiness repels bacteria and protects against skin damage. It also helps to waterproof the skin; a dry skin easily cracks and becomes prone to infection as well as becoming very sticky and irritating due to a leaking out of subcutaneous tissue fluids.

In acne, however, the sebum becomes over-thick. We know that the stickiness factor of sebum (its viscosity) is influenced by hormones circulating in the blood (notably the predominantly male hormone testosterone, a substance also produced in women). But testosterone is not the only factor involved in sebum secretion. A group of scientists set up an experiment that actually measured the rate of sebum production on the face under two conditions. The first was during periods of tranquillity. During this period sebum production was remarkably stable. But during periods of stress in which feelings of anger were artificially induced into the test situation, greatly increased sebum production occurred.

These simple dermatological facts tell us a lot about acne. In adolescence and young adult life, testosterone makes the sebum very sticky and so instead of gradually being eased out of the sebaceous glands, like toothpaste on to a brush, it tends to remain in these glands making them swell (into a blackhead) and then burst into the tissues around the hair follicles. This ultimately causes the acne spot. Under conditions of stress the whole process is compounded. Not only is the hormone-produced sticky sebum difficult to shift, but the stress-produced excess sebum provides an extra hazard for the skin to contend with. Thus acne and stress become closely linked, and the fact that a girl's acne is always worse when she wants to look at her best is easily understood.

With acne the very nature of the appearance of the disease further complicates the psychological picture. It makes the victim resentful (why am I like this when she looks beautiful?), withdrawn (suppressed anger), and feel inferior. Good medical treatment will help with the sticky sebum aspect of acne. Learning to relax will slowly but relentlessly and surely diminish the stress factors and help the skin to improve naturally too. Dermatologists will often state blandly that acne is cured by marriage. Really they are saying that when the tense and adolescent girl settles down to a more relaxed life as a young bride then her skin will impove.

Thoughtful doctors are much less liable to label their difficult skin patients as 'neurotic' these days. When eczema, dermatitis, and even in some people psoriasis, seem intractable or recurrent an examination of the sufferer's stress load or anxiety quotient may be much more important than changing the ointment they use on their skin. By learning to relax many patients with difficult complexions first of all find the projection of their nervous system (the skin) is less difficult to cope with. Later their skin usually starts to behave itself, reflecting the state of their more relaxed inner self, and instead of battling with a skin problem they allow their body as a whole to ease it better.

Asthma and migraine

Asthma and migraine might seem to be two strange illnesses to link together but there is an increasing amount of evidence to say that similar causative factors are involved.

One way to look at asthma is to think of it as a change in the body's functioning that is brought about by a simple combination of changes in the environment. First of all there is an asthmatic constitution; some people tend to get wheezy from time to time and others don't. Usually we find that more than one factor is involved in the production of an asthmatic attack, and in all cases stress is involved. Often two types of stress have to be experienced by the asthma-prone individual before he gets wheezy. The common stress factors are infection and allergy, although stress from other forms can also trigger an attack – for instance, exercise or emotional disturbance. In many cases the asthmatic reaction seems to be put on alert by one form of stress – shall we say by an infection, a cold – and while in this sensitive state a second form of stress – perhaps contact with an allergy-producing factor or even a change in environmental temperature – will trigger the classic symptoms of wheezing and breathlessness.

What holds for asthma also holds for migraine. Migraine can be triggered by the eating of certain foods, by flashing lights, by the observation of disturbing patterns. Changes in the emotions of a stressful nature are also liable to trigger off a migraine.

In both migraine and asthma it might be said that the body is over-sensitive to stress and that an increase in stress moves the victim a little bit further towards experiencing an attack of his symptoms. Learning to reduce stress will obviously be of enormous help in coping with these problems.

Resistance to colds

Exactly how we catch colds is a mystery. Possibly 200 different viruses are involved, but it is often very difficult to persuade a victim to 'catch cold' experimentally even though the virus is introduced in quite large quantities into his nose or naso-pharynx.

Folklore warns us about getting 'chilled to the bone', and there is no doubt at all that in reducing the body's temperature we also reduce its resistance to infection. This is probably mediated by the stress hormones that I have mentioned previously (see page 98). It seems highly likely that stressful situations reduce the body's resistance to all sorts of diseases including those caused by viruses and bacteria. And so learning to cope with stress can mean that the victim of 'cold after cold' can obtain unexpected relief.

Cancer and stress

There are complex if rather ill-defined relationships between stress and the development of various forms of cancer. This is based on the concept of cancer being an on-going dynamic condition throughout the whole body in which, during the normal process of tissue repair and regeneration, abnormal precancerous cells spontaneously evolve. In the normal state of affairs the body's immune system, which is primarily concerned with our resistance to infection, rapidly scavenges and destroys these abnormal cells. In the same way in which adverse environmental conditions – for example extreme cold – can depress the body's immune system, thereby allowing infections to occur apparently spontaneously, another stress-induced reaction by our immune system can allow pre-malignant cells to 'get away' and therefore develop separate entities within the body which eventually come to light as one form of cancer or another.

It would be a brave man who could put his hand on his heart and say that the relaxation response can prevent cancer; nevertheless, it does seem highly probable that the development of cancer and chronic stress are in some way closely linked together.

Relaxation and the special problems of women

Women get ill rather more frequently than men. They go to the doctor more often, yet on the whole they are fitter than men and they live considerably longer. This is not really such a paradox as it would seem. The more frequent consultation rate in women is related to medical problems that arise in relation to reproductive function. This, with its inherent hormone domination of the system, is largely responsible for the symptoms that make medical consultations relatively frequent during the fertile life. But the female sex hormones also have a vast and inexplicable protective effect on the health of women – particularly on their cardiovascular system, their blood pressure and their heart. It could be said that when a women enters a menopause, say at 50, her hormones have given her at least a decade or two of health protection over the years. (Some years ago when doctors began to realize this they started prescribing female sex hormones to men who had suffered coronary artery disease. Such unfortunate men soon began to grow breasts and become feminized. But it did not solve their medical problems. For that to have happened the hormones would have have had to been started some 20 years previously.)

Stress and anxiety have several rather special female connotations and the relaxation respose is well geared to help in such cases. It is always difficult to separate *soma* (body) from *pysche* (spirit), and to some extent these difficulties become compounded when a *man* endeavours to draw conclusions about what is, after all, a strictly female entity – the female psyche. But it should be possible to trace some widely accepted circuits in the life of women that explain how stress and tension can interfere with body function without raising too many cries of 'sexist'. The following scenario takes into consideration the known scientific facts.

BASIC PERSONALITY TYPE

It is hardly necessary to state that women, like men, have certain inborn characteristics with reference to their *psyche*. Women may be emotionally mature or immature, dependent or independent. Each of these four intrinsic factors has to react with general stress situations, the most common of which are sibling rivalry, social, economic and occupational pressures, marital or emotional hazards and, of course, the competitive pressures common to the existence of both sexes. The result of such reactions produces, as it does in men, various degrees of unresolved conflict and naturally related anxiety.

Anxiety in both sexes produces changes in the body's automatic (autonomic) nervous system. These can be common to both sexes (for example bladder irritability, stomach and bowel upsets) or sex specific. In both sexes the anxiety and stress-disturbed function of the autonomic centre in the brain brings about *local* effects in the body (characterized in women by changes in blood supply to the pelvic organs); *general* effects in women are brought about by a disturbance of the function of the pituitary gland, and the adrenal glands on the ovaries.

Another way of saying this is to state that there is an increased potential in women – because of their intrinsic femininity – to be subject to stress. And this stress operates in women in a rather more diffuse way than it does in men. Episodes of ill health in women are associated very much with their femaleness.

The following all produce their own tension load:

1. The general emotional upheaval of the menarche and the menopause.

2. Pregnancy-related unhappiness (too many, too few).

3. Menstrual disturbances (painful, irregular, heavy periods).

4. Premenstrual tension.

5. Sexual problems.

Medical solutions to these female conditions can be considerable and valuable. But seldom are they, on their own, totally satisfactory. One reason for this only partial medical solution resides in a more or less intrinsically female method of dealing with many such problems. In our culture it is far more acceptable for women to obtain a secondary gain through illness than it is for men. Thus 'being ill' often produces for the female *psyche* increased sympathy and attention, which can be *manna* indeed for the dependent or immature personality. This would not matter if it were not the case that such an innate state of affairs tends to lead to further disturbance of the emotional equilibrium and thus compounds the basic problem.

A judicious use of the relaxation response can help enormously in the problems of anxiety by interrupting the chain of events that aggravates female problems at the very centre of automatic (autonomic) activity. In the same way as the combination of pendulum-type breathing and muscular relaxation influence other autonomic functions such as the blood pressure and the heart rate, they can also alter the central discharge of nervous impulses to the master glands of femininity, the pituitary, the adrenal glands and the ovaries. These in turn then function properly; malfunction of these glands is a major factor in the development of female complaints at all ages.

The relaxation response has been proved of value in the management of disorders of menstruation, fertility problems, the emotional and physical problems of adolescence, and the menopause. It also helps with a wide variety of sexual problems. Always in such cases accurate medical diagnosis is a prerequisite of treatment and management.

Conditions in which upset autonomic function (stress) aggravates or produces physical symptoms

CONDITION	PROBABLE MECHANISM
Dysmenorrhoea (painful periods)	Cramp-like contraction of uterine muscles
Menorrhagia (heavy periods)	Changes in coagulability of blood
PMT (premenstrual tension)	? direct hormone effect
Dyspareunia (painful intercourse)	'fight or flight' reaction with loss of vaginal lubrication
Menopause	Direct hormone effect on blood vessels
Missed periods (amenorrhoea)	Inhibition of pituitary function
Lack of sexual drive or interest	Inhibition of pituitary function plus 'fight of flight' mechanisms

Stress and the special problems of men

Certain forms of secondary impotence in men (impotence developing in a man who has previously been able to perform sexually quite adequately) are stress-induced. Many of the classical forms of sex therapy, for instance those advocated by Masters and Johnson, really boil down to the male sex partner losing the various anxiety tags that have attached themselves to his sexual performance, during which he seems to observe, as a spectator might do, his sexual activities. The Masters and Johnson so-called *sensate focusing* is in many ways a modified touching and massage technique in which both partners relearn how to enjoy physical contact rather than looking upon it as a stressful exercise with a definite goal – i.e. sexual intercourse.

In many cases sexual anxiety can be very much diminished by following a 'Relax with a friend' type of programme (see Chapter 9).

Anxiety and Depression, Prof. Robert Priest, *Martin Dunitz*
The Good Health Guide, *Pan*
Insomnia, Dr. Peter Tyrer, *Sheldon Press*
Release from Nervous Tension, Dr. D. H. Fink, *Allen & Unwin*
The Relaxation Response Dr. Herbert Benson, *Avon*
Self Help for your Nerves, Dr. Claire Weekes, *Angus & Robertson*
Stress and Relaxation, Jane Madders, *Martin Dunitz*
Taking the Strain, Robert Eagle, *BBC Publications*

Recommended
reading

Useful addresses

The Alexander Technique
3b Albert Court,
Prince Consort Road,
London S.W.7.

The Centre for Autogenic Training
12 Milford House,
7 Queen Anne Street,
London W.1.

Look After Yourself Project Centre
Health Education Council,
Christchurch College,
Canterbury,
Kent.

National Childbirth Trust
9 Queensborough Terrace,
London W.2.

Relaxation for Living
29 Burwood Park Road,
Walton on Thames,
Surrey.
(*Information can be supplied only on receipt of a s.a.e.*)

Maharishi Majesh Yogi
Capital of the Age of Enlightenment,
Royden Hall,
Seven Mile Lane,
East Peckham,
Tonbridge,
Kent.